Making Decorative
Lawn Ornaments
& Patio Containers

SAGE

Making Decorative Lawn Ornaments & Patio Containers

Edie Stockstill

Sterling Publishing Co., Inc. New York
A Sterling/Chapelle Book

For Chapelle Ltd.
Owner: Jo Packham
Editor: Cherie Hanson
Staff: Trice Boerens, Malissa Boatwright, Rebecca Christensen, Holly Fuller, Holly Hollingsworth, Susan Jorgenson, Susan Laws, Amanda McPeck, Jamie Pierce, Leslie Ridenour, Cindy Stoeckl, Nancy Whitley, and Lorrie Young
Photographer: Kevin Dilley for Hazen Photography

Fountain designed by Mike Lee and Ron Tribe.

A special thank you to Jo Packham, Leo and Sheri Wohler, Dale and Stacey Campbell, Janice Barton, and Mr. and Mrs. Wheeler for allowing us to photograph at their homes and gardens.

For information on where to purchase specialty items in this book, please write to: Chapelle Ltd. Customer Service Department, P.O. Box 9252, Ogden, Ut 84409.

Library of Congress Cataloging-in-Publication Data

Stockstill, Edie.
Making decorative lawn ornaments & patio containers / by Edie Stockstill.
p. cm.
"A Sterling/Chapelle book."
Includes index.
ISBN 0-8069-1290-1
1. Woodwork—Amateur's manuals. 2. Garden ornaments and furniture—Design and construction—Amateur's manuals. 3. Plant containers—Design and construction—Amateur's manuals. 4. Painted woodwork—Amateur's manuals. I. Title. II. Title: Making decorative lawn ornaments and patio containers.
TT185.S76 1994 94-49353
684.1'8—dc20 CIP

A Sterling/Chapelle Book

1 3 5 7 9 10 8 6 4 2

First paperback edition published in 1995 by
Sterling Publishing Company, Inc.
387 Park Avenue South, New York, N.Y. 10016
Produced by Chapelle Ltd.
P.O. Box 9252, Newgate Station, Ogden, Utah 84409

Distributed in Canada by Sterling Publishing
℅ Canadian Manda Group, One Atlantic Avenue, Suite 105
Toronto, Ontario, Canada M6K 3E7
Distributed in Great Britain and Europe by Cassell PLC
Wellington House, 125 Strand, London WC2R 0BB, England
Distributed in Australia by Capricorn Link (Australia) Pty Ltd.
P.O. Box 6651, Baulkham Hills, Business Centre, NSW 2153, Australia
Printed in Hong Kong

Sterling ISBN 0-8069-1290-1 Trade
0-8069-1291-X Paper

Preface

If you love to decorate your yard and garden, you will enjoy this book of wonderful wooden pieces that celebrate each season and the holidays within. Gardening can be done year round by placing plants in patio containers that can be transferred to a sunny window indoors when the snow falls.

First comes Spring, a most alluring season for any gardener. Little green buds of perennials pushing up through the warming ground and sunny beds of tulips and daffodils inspire creativity. What a perfect time for making some colorful wooden Easter eggs for the lawn, or building a unique planter for an umbrella table for a special Spring luncheon.

Then there is Summer, when the garden and lawn are in their full glory. This is the perfect time to plant a dramatic, yet terribly easy, tiered jardiniere for your patio. Also, a book of lawn ornaments would not be complete without some playful flamingos strutting around the lawn.

Crisp mornings and brilliant colors herald Autumn. The scarecrow in this chapter is one of my favorites. Every Halloween he comes out of the garden and sits by my front door, surrounded by wooden pumpkins to greet trick or treaters.

Winter means snow and lots of fun outdoors. Snow-covered rolling hills and mountain trails are great places for kids of all ages to sled. All of which inspired the sled found in this chapter. It is a perfect planter for winter, decorated with pinecones and an evergreen tree. Winter also means Christmas and a beautiful way to decorate your lawn is a life-sized elegant gold-leafed Santa Claus. His robe is hand-painted with tiny golden reindeer and holly.

You will find many ways to decorate your lawn and patio for all the seasons with the many projects that follow. Have fun and happy holidays.

–Edie Stockstill

Contents

Chapter One
Spring

Chapter Two
Summer

Chapter Three
Autumn

Chapter Four
Winter

General Instructions

Tracing and Transferring

- Materials and tools you will need include tracing paper, transfer paper, a pencil, a photocopy machine if necessary, and drafting tape.

- Lay tracing paper on top of your pattern and trace pattern.

- If directions indicate enlarging a pattern, place pattern directly in photocopy machine. Set the photocopy machine to percentage required and enlarge. A few projects in this book need to be enlarged 400% and some photocopy machines do not enlarge that much. To do this, enlarge the pattern 200%, using this enlarged pattern, enlarge 200% again

- Tape traced or photocopied pattern in position on the surface of the object to be cut or painted.

- Insert a piece of transfer paper between pattern and the object. Trace over pattern, transferring marks to object.

Because tracing paper is thin enough to see through, it allows you to retrace the original pattern lines easily. Transfer paper is coated on one side with graphite or chalk. When you press on it with a pencil, it transfers the graphite or chalk to the surface under it. Since transfer paper is coated on only one side, make a small mark and determine if you have the correct side down.

Transfer paper comes in a variety of colors, which is helpful when working on different colored backgrounds. For instance, black graphite works well on unfinished pine, but white or yellow would be easier to see on dark green surfaces.

Painting

Materials you will need include acrylic paints, 1/4", and 1" flat artist's brushes, a #2 round liner brush, and a 2" utility paintbrush.

Artist's brushes are called flat or round; this refers to the shape of the metal part of the brush that holds the bristles onto the shaft. Brushes are numbered as well; the higher the number, the larger the brush. A size 10 flat for instance will be about an inch across, a size 5 is more like a half an inch. A size 3 or #2 round is very small and is used for fine line work and details.

Most of the painting on projects in this book are done in a simple country style. After you have traced and transferred the patterns, fill in with the background color first, then go back and paint fine detail lines, retracing them if necessary. It should really be like coloring in a coloring book, just stay within the lines.

Most projects require a base coat. This is the background color. Since this is usually a fairly good-sized area, a larger brush makes for a faster job.

There is very little blending or shading on these projects, but in a few places a technique called double loading was used. Dip one-half of a flat artist's brush in one color, and the other half in a different color. Take a couple of test strokes in the same place. The brush blends the colors for you. Now stroke it across your design and you will see a blended look.

Some designs are made up of dots. Dots are, of course, small circles filled in and you may paint them this way, but a simple technique is to dip the end of your paintbrush or similar-sized object such as a pencil eraser, and use it like a stamp to make the dot.

Acrylic paint cleans up with soap and water when still wet. Be sure to clean your brushes thoroughly with soap and water until the water runs clear. Never leave your brushes standing in water overnight. It will soften the glue that holds the bristles and bend them out of shape.

No matter how careful you are, it is always a good idea to use a drop cloth , old newspapers, or something to protect your work areas. Acrylic paint will wipe right up off a nonporous surface like tile or linoleum or it will even peel off when dry. But acrylic paint on carpet will soak in immediately and probably not come completely clean. It is best in this case if it is a small amount, to let the paint dry and cut it from the top of the carpet. Clothing too will probably be ruined by acrylic paint. It is recommended when working with acrylic paint to use a drop cloth and wear old clothes.

Woodworking

Most of the projects in this book are cut with a hand-held electric jigsaw, which works well for 1"-thick pine. Some of the more advanced projects, such as the umbrella table and porch swing, require a table saw or any type of saw that can cut through the thicker 2" x 4" pieces of wood. Of course, the projects could be cut with hand saws, but this is much slower and requires more effort.

Any project in this book that requires the use of power tools is an intermediate to advanced level project.

The following are some safety tips every woodworker should keep in mind.

- Read and understand all instructions that accompany your power tools.
- Always wear safety glasses or goggles. Even when your tool has a blade guard, small pieces of wood sometimes splinter off.
- Use clamps, not your hands, to hold the wood in place. Never allow your hands to come near the cutting blade. It is recommended to keep both hands on top of the saw handle. Leaving your hand on the wood could result in accidentally cutting into your hand.
- Before working with a tool for the first time, ask for pointers and assistance from someone who is familiar with that tool.

About cutting circles:
When you need to cut out circles or shapes in the middle of a board, you need to first drill a hole in the part you want to cut out. The hole needs to be large enough for the saw blade to fit into (about 1/4"). After you have drilled the hole, put your blade into the hole and proceed just as on the edge of the board.

To attach bases:
Turn base upside down. Set the project on the base. Center and mark the base position by tracing around project. Remove the project from the base. Drill two countersunk holes within the marks. Turn the project upside down. Set the base on the bottom of the project, checking marks. Attach base to project with wood screws.

The following are some basic jigsaw instructions.

- After tracing the pattern onto the wood, clamp the board to a worktable with at least two large clamps. The pattern and wood should hang over the edge far enough that the wood can be cut but not so close that you cut into your worktable. Cut approximately a foot at a time, moving and reclamping as you go. If too much of the wood hangs over the edge, you will have too much vibration. Experiment with your clamps and tools to determine what works best for you.

- Start on the outside edge of the board. Put your saw feet on the board but DO NOT let the blade touch the board. Turn the saw on and slowly ease the moving blade into the wood.

- Move the saw slowly, following the lines you have traced. When going around corners and other tight turns, go very slowly and let the blade do the work.

- Make certain you replace blades when they become dull. A dull blade will break or cut very slowly.

- Be careful cutting through knots in the wood. They are very hard and difficult to cut through. Try to avoid putting cutting lines through knots wherever possible.

- When you reach a very tight turn, back up a half an inch and make a second cut slightly outside the one you are trying to make. When you join the second path to the original, it cuts a small piece of wood out, allowing you room to turn the blade and complete the cut.

- If you use a fine wood cutting blade, you will get a clean cut, but when necessary, sand any rough edges.

About Lumber

Dimensions for lumber are written with the thickness first and width second; for example, 1" x 12" means that the board is 1" thick and 12" wide. The next measurement tells how long the board is.

However, if you actually measure a board, you will find the dimensions are slightly smaller. This is a result of surfacing or planing at the lumber mill to remove the roughness of raw lumber. This makes no difference when using the lumber, so do not be alarmed if your boards do not “measure up”.

Antiquing

The same method is used for both antiquing and whitewashing surfaces. The only difference is the color of the paint in the original mix.

The materials and tools you will need are burnt umber artist's oil paint for antiquing or white artist's oil paint for whitewashing, paint thinner, oil-based varnish, a 2" utility paintbrush, a bowl or other small container to mix paint, and plastic gloves which are optional.

- Mix equal parts of artist's oil paint, paint thinner, and oil-based varnish. Most projects take about 2–4 tablespoons of each.

- Apply mixture to surface of project with a rag or 2" utility paintbrush.

- Wipe off excess before it sets up (usually within five minutes depending on the temperature).

- The more stain you leave on, the more antiqued or whitewashed your project will look. You can always reapply more stain after a piece dries, but you cannot remove dried stain.

Copper Patina

Materials you will need include flat black spray paint, light turquoise acrylic paint, metallic copper acrylic paint, bowl or other small container to mix paint, 2" utility paintbrush, and rags.

Spray-paint your project completely black. Allow to dry.

In a bowl, thin the light turquoise paint with water to make a wash. A 1:1 ratio works well. Paint small sections at a time with thinned paint. Immediately wipe off the excess paint with a rag. The paint dries quickly, so only paint what you can manage in a one to three minute interval. The ratio of paint to water, and the amount you choose to wipe off, will determine whether your pieces will be more patina or more wrought iron. Allow paint to dry thoroughly.

Using the metallic copper acrylic paint, highlight portions of your pieces. Apply small amounts of paint to a finger or rag and lightly touch and rub the places you want to accent.

Gold Leafing

Materials you will need include reddish-brown acrylic paint, spray adhesive, sheets of gold leafing, and a small paintbrush.

- Unless already a reddish-brown color, paint pieces with a coat of reddish-brown acrylic paint. Allow to dry.

- Spray pieces with adhesive, allowing it to set a minute before proceeding.

- Apply the gold leaf, one sheet at a time. Brush gently with a dry paintbrush so that the gold leaf adheres to the surface. Remember that the first time the leaf touches the adhesive, it is permanent. If you do not get as complete coverage as you want, apply more gold leaf.

- Allow adhesive and leafing to dry completely, usually about 24 hours.

Chapter One

Spring

Rose Umbrella Planter

Materials

One 2" x 6" piece of redwood, 5½ feet long
Twenty-four 2¼" wood screws
One 15" x 15" piece of exterior grade plywood, ¾" thick
One 5" length of 2"-diameter PVC pipe
5½ ounces of clear silicone sealant caulk
Wood putty
Light green, white, mauve, dark green, light blue, medium blue, yellow, rust, gray, olive green, and purple acrylic paints
Four wood finials
Exterior varnish
Antiquing supplies

Tools

Table saw
#2 Phillips screwdriver or drill with #2 Phillips screw bit
Countersink bit
2" wood drill bit
Pencil
Putty knife
Sandpaper
2" utility paintbrush
1" flat artist's brush
¼" flat artist's brush
#2 round liner artist's brush
Tracing paper
Transfer paper
Bowl or small container to mix paint

Directions

1. Cut two 15" and two 18" pieces of 2" x 6" redwood for the box.

2. Lay out the pieces of the box as shown in the diagram. Attach the longer sides to the shorter sides with two wood screws at each joint. Be sure to predrill the screw hole locations with your countersink bit.

3. Drill a 2"-diameter hole in the center of the plywood bottom. To locate the center, draw an "X" from corner to corner. The center will be the intersection of the lines; see diagram.

4. Attach plywood bottom to the bottom of the box with two countersunk screws running through each side of the box.

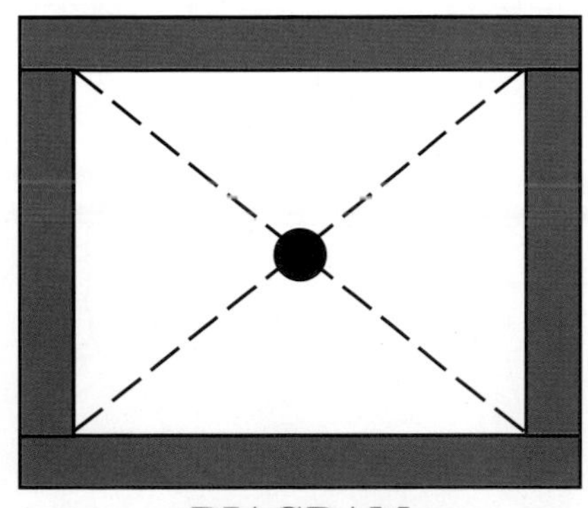

DIAGRAM

5. Putty and sand all countersunk screw locations.

6. Put the PVC pipe over center hole and caulk with sealant. Caulk all interior seams of the box.

7. Paint box with a base coat of light green paint; allow to dry.

8. Trace and transfer umbrella patterns, found on pages 16 and 17, for each side of the box; see "Tracing and Transferring" on page 8.

9. Paint patterns and finials; refer to patterns and photo.

10. Antique; see "Antiquing" on page 10.

11. Seal entire box with exterior varnish. Allow to dry. Screw finials on each corner of planter.

Yard Birds

Materials

One 1" x 12" piece of pine wood, 2 feet long
Red, orange, green yellow, black, white, and blue acrylic paint
Burnt umber wood stain
Exterior varnish
One 3/8" wooden dowel, 3 feet long
Wood glue

Tools

Tracing paper
Graphite or transfer paper
Pencil
Jigsaw
Drill with 1/4" drill bit
Wood clamps
Sandpaper
Hammer

Directions

1. Trace pattern of one bird, found on page 20, and transfer it to the 1" x 12" pine; see "Tracing and Transferring" on page 8.

2. Cut out bird from pine; see "Woodworking" on page 9.

3. Using the wooden bird as a pattern, trace five more birds. Cut birds out.

4. Paint each bird with a base coat of acrylic paint; see pattern and photo.

5. Transfer the details on each bird; see "Tracing and Transferring" on page 8.

6. Paint details. Allow to dry. Remember to paint all sides of the birds because they will be seen from all sides.

7. Antique birds with burnt umber stain; see "Antiquing" on page 10.

8. Cut dowel into six assorted lengths, ranging between one and two feet.

9. Drill a 1/4" hole in the bottom of each bird. To make the birds tip in different directions, vary the location and direction of the drilled holes. This gives the birds the look of feeding, landing, or just looking around.

10. Put a dab of wood glue in each hole and insert dowel. Tap dowel firmly in place with a hammer. The hole should be smaller than the dowel to ensure a tight fit.

11. Seal with exterior varnish.

These birds look great everywhere—in the yard and garden, in large whiskey barrel planters, on fence posts, or even perched on outdoor furniture. Be creative! For example, paint all the birds black. It will look as if a flock of crows has landed in your yard.

YARD BIRDS PATTERNS

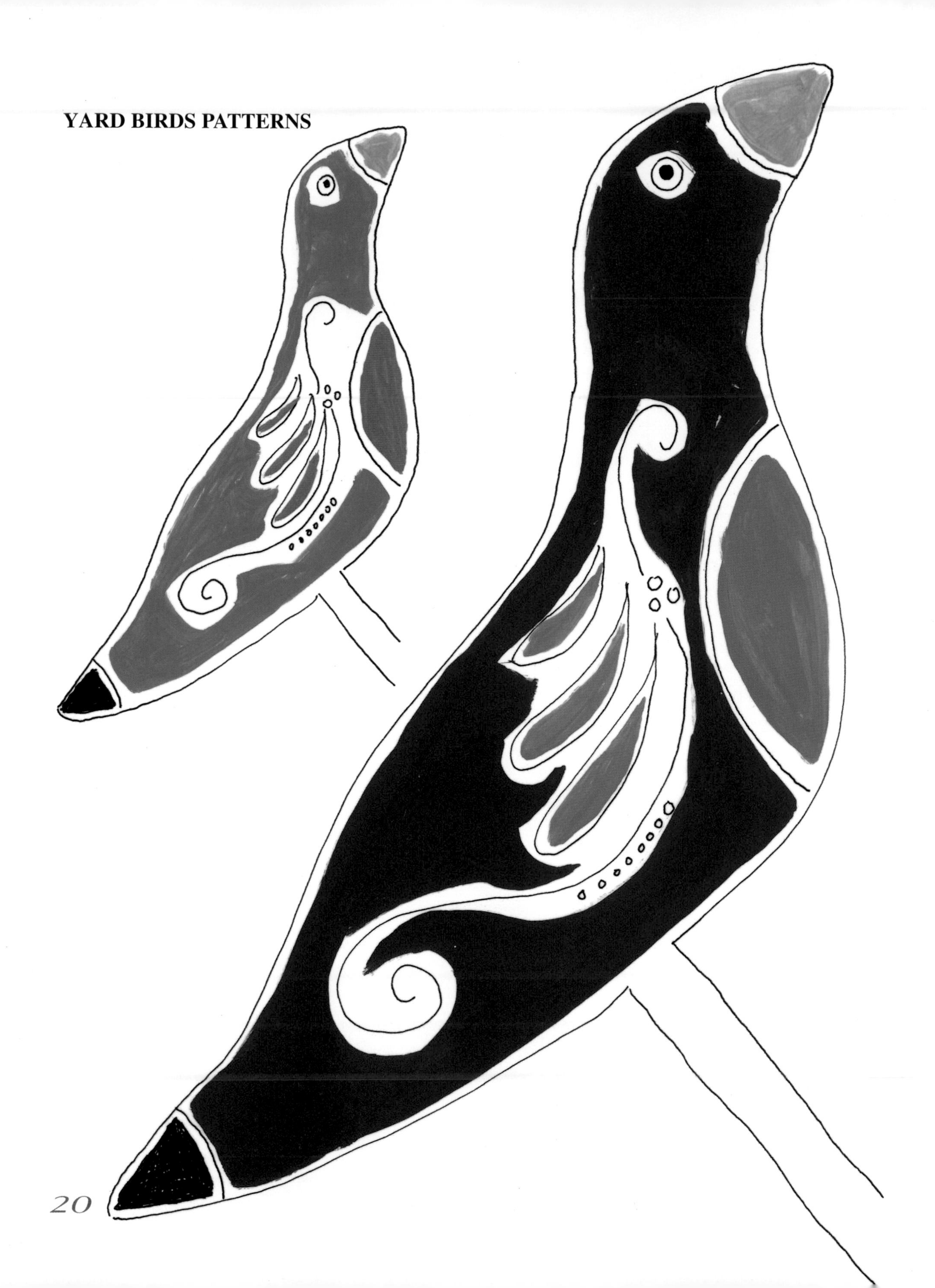

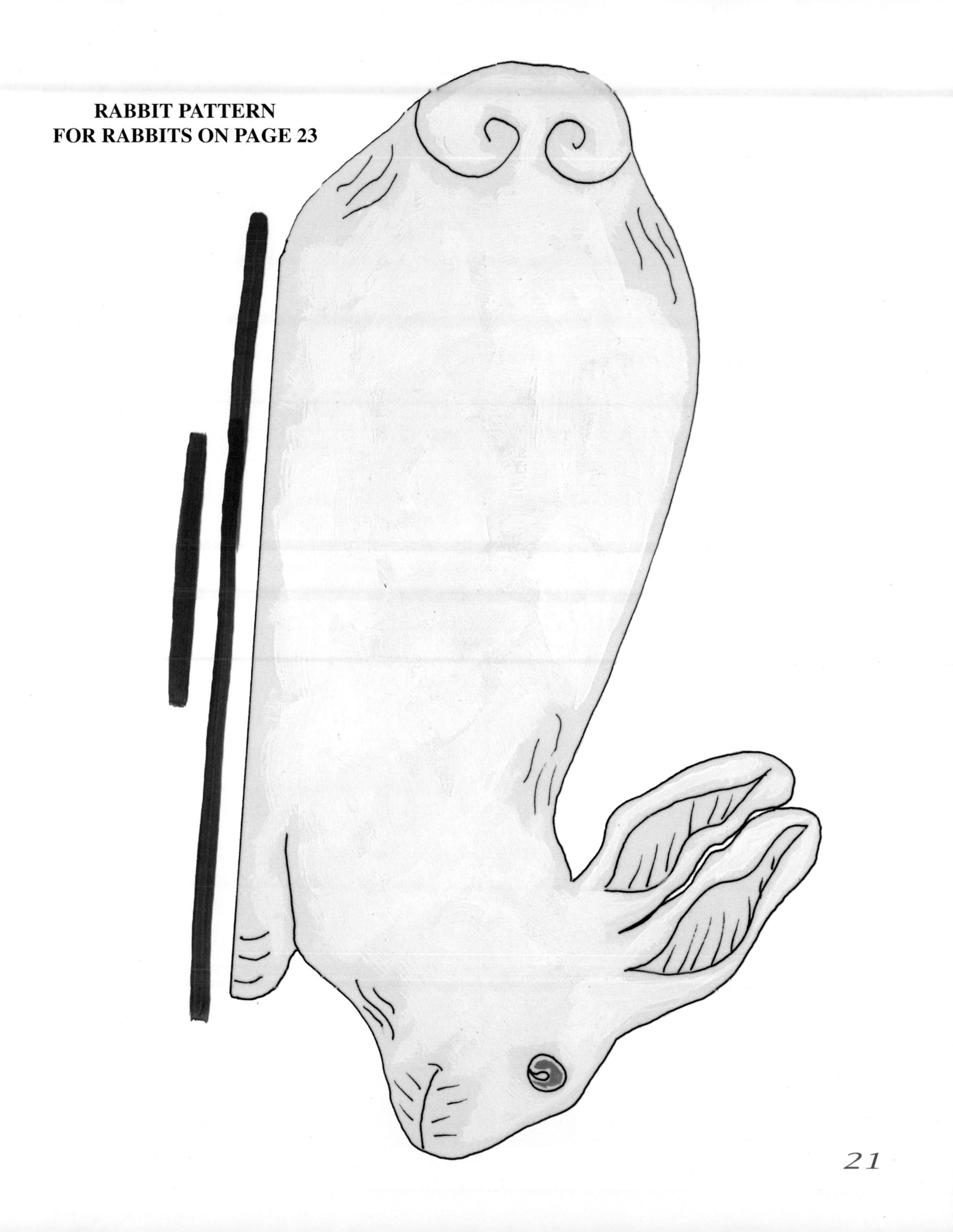

RABBIT PATTERN
FOR RABBITS ON PAGE 23

Rabbits

Materials

One 1" x 12" piece of pine wood, 4 1/2 feet long
White, green, yellow, and black acrylic paint
Four 1 1/2" wood screws
Exterior varnish
Burnt umber artist's oil color
Paint thinner
Oil-based varnish
7 feet of variegated wired ribbon

Tools

Photocopy machine
Tracing paper
Transfer paper
Pencil
Jigsaw
Wood clamps
Sandpaper
Drill with countersink bit
Phillips screwdriver or drill with phillips bit
2" utility paintbrush
#2 round artist's liner brush
Rags
Bowl or other small container to mix paint
Scissors

Directions

1. Using a photocopy machine, enlarge rabbit patterns, found on pages 21 and 24, 400%. Transfer enlarged patterns to 1" x 12" pine; see "Tracing and Transferring" on page 8.

2. Cut out rabbits; see "Woodworking" on page 9.

3. For the tall rabbit, cut a 12" x 3 1/2" base from pine; cut a 15" x 3 1/2" base for the short rabbit.

4. Sand edges of wood as necessary.

5. Paint rabbits with a base coat of white acrylic paint. Allow to dry.

6. Paint bases with a base coat of green acrylic paint. Allow to dry.

7. Trace and transfer details onto rabbits; see "Tracing and Transferring" on page 8.

8. Paint eyes yellow. Allow to dry.

9. Using round liner brush, paint details black. Allow to dry.

10. Attach rabbits to bases; see "Woodworking" on page 9.

11. Antique rabbits and bases; see "Antiquing" on page 10.

12. Seal rabbits with exterior varnish.

13. Cut ribbon into two equal lengths. Tie a bow around each rabbit's neck.

These little rabbits are darling in your yard and garden and they won't ever nibble on your plants!

RABBIT PATTERN

COPPER PLANTER PLAQUE PATTERN FOR COPPER PLANTER PLAQUE ON PAGE 27

Copper Planter Plaque

Materials

One 1" x 12" piece of pine wood, 2 feet long
White, light green, and dark green acrylic paint
Burnt umber artist's oil paint
Paint thinner
Oil-based varnish
Exterior varnish
One wrought iron and copper hanging planter
One 2" nail

Tools

Photocopy machine
Tracing paper
Transfer paper
Pencil
Jigsaw
Wood clamps
Sandpaper
Bowl or other small container to mix paint
2" flat utility paintbrush
1/4" flat artist's paint brush
#2 round liner artist's brush
Rags
Hammer

Directions

1. Using a photocopy machine, enlarge plaque pattern, found on page 25, 200%. Transfer plaque pattern to 1" x 12" pine; see "Tracing and Transferring" on page 8.

2. Cut out plaque; see "Woodworking" on page 9.

3. Sand edges of wood as necessary.

4. Paint plaque with a base coat of white acrylic paint. Allow to dry.

5. Trace and transfer leaves and vines; see "Tracing and Transferring" on page 8.

6. Paint half of each leaf light green and the other half dark green; see pattern and photo.

7. Using liner brush, paint vines. Allow to dry.

8. Antique plaque; see "Antiquing" on page 10.

9. Seal with exterior varnish.

10. Hammer a small nail to top of plaque. Hang planter from nail.

Dress up any ordinary planter or protect walls that come in contact with metal planters from permanent rust marks with this beautiful painted plaque.

CAUTION
XING

Geese

Materials

One 1" x 12" piece of pine wood, 9 feet long
White, green, peach, and black acrylic paint
Four 1 1/2" wood screws
Exterior varnish
Burnt umber artist's oil color
Paint thinner
Oil-based varnish
Three 6"-diameter grapevine wreaths
Eighteen dried rosebuds
Purple statice
3 feet of yellow ribbon

Tools

Photocopy machine
Tracing paper
Transfer paper
Pencil
Jigsaw
Wood clamps
Sandpaper
Drill with countersink bit
2" utility paintbrush
1/4" flat artist's brush
Rags
Bowl or other small container to mix paint
Scissors
Hot glue gun with glue sticks

Directions

1. Using a photocopy machine, enlarge geese patterns, found on pages 30 and 31, 400%. Transfer enlarged patterns to 1" x 12" pine; see "Tracing and Transferring" on page 8.

2. Cut out geese; see "Woodworking" on page 9.

3. Cut three 12" x 3 1/2" pieces of pine for bases; see "Woodworking" on page 9.

4. Sand edges of wood as necessary.

5. Paint geese with a base coat of white acrylic paint. Allow to dry.

6. Paint bases with a base coat of green acrylic paint. Allow to dry.

7. Trace and transfer details onto geese; see "Tracing and Transferring" on page 8.

8. Paint beaks and feet peach; paint eyes black. Allow to dry.

9. Attach geese to the bases; see "Woodworking" on page 9.

10. Antique geese and bases; see "Antiquing" on page 10.

11. Seal geese with exterior varnish.

12. Hot-glue rosebuds and statice to grapevine wreaths.

13. Cut ribbon into three 12" lengths.

14. Knot one length of ribbon around each wreath.

15. Put one wreath around each goose's neck.

These geese are an all time favorite. They look great all year round. In winter, they trade their wreaths for Christmas bows.

GEESE PATTERN

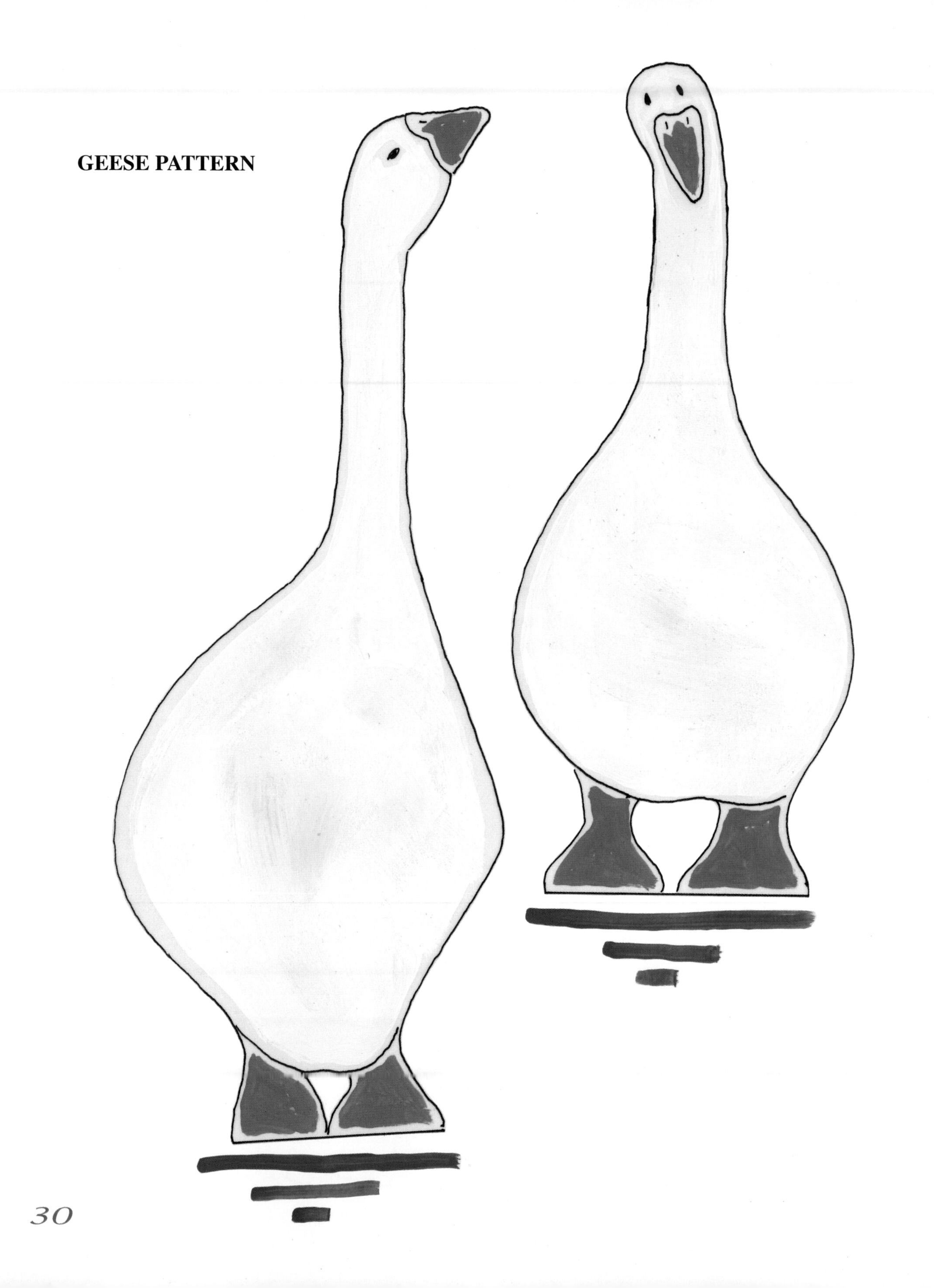

GEESE PATTERN

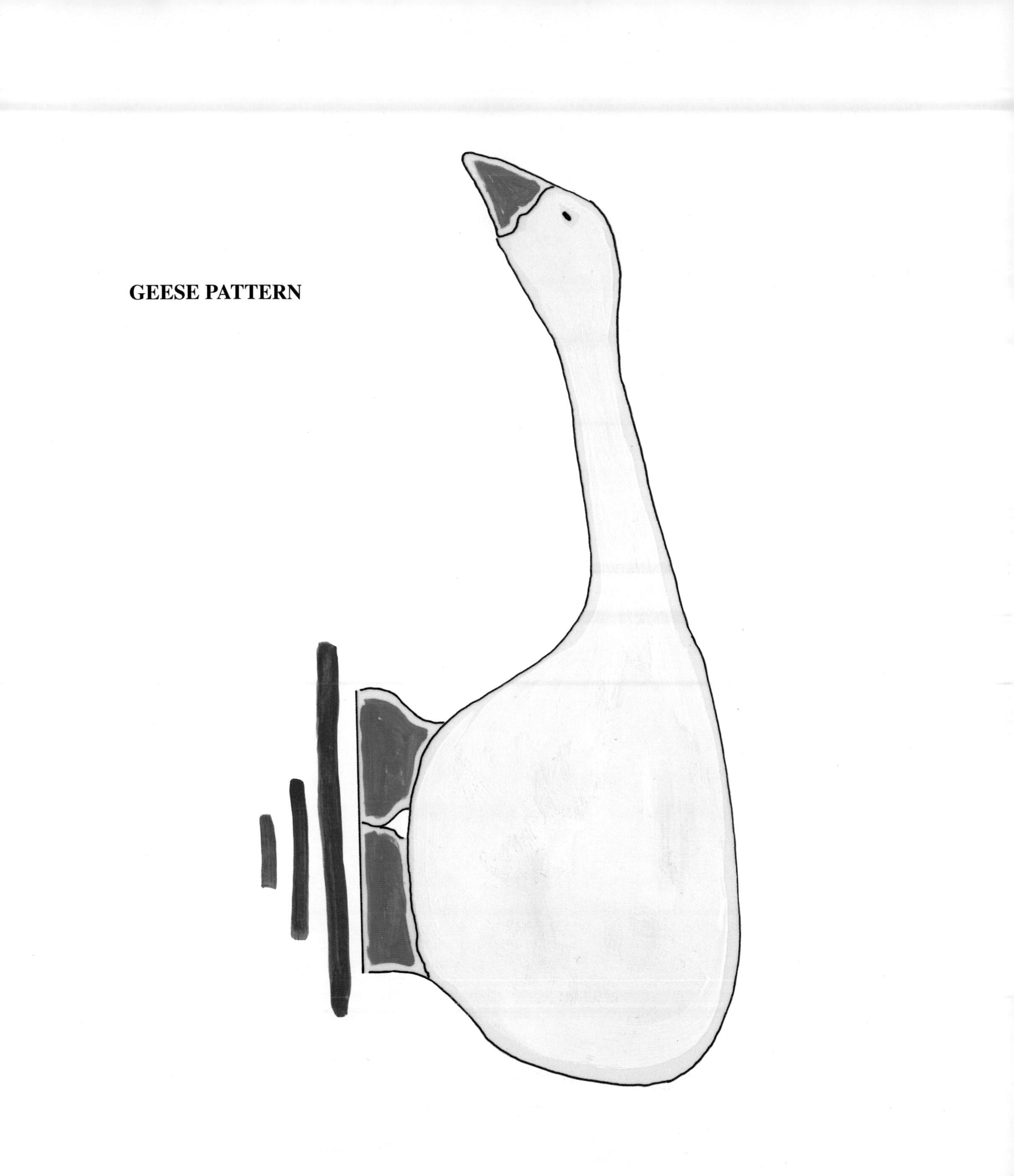

Gar"D"en Angel

Materials

One 1" x 12" piece of pine wood, 5 feet long
One 1" x 2" piece of pine wood, 6 feet long
Light blue, white, ivory, peach, mauve, dark green, tan, yellow, orange, and brown acrylic paint
Burnt umber artist's oil color
Paint thinner
Oil-based varnish
Exterior varnish
Seven $1^1/_4$" wood screws

Tools

Photocopy machine
Tracing paper
Transfer paper
Pencil
Jigsaw
Wood clamps
Sandpaper
Ruler or straight edge
Drill with #2 phillips screw driver bit
Bowl or other small container to mix paint
Rags
1" flat artist's brush
$^1/_4$" flat artist's brush
#2 round liner artist's brush

Directions

1. Using a photocopy machine, enlarge angel and wing patterns, found on pages 34 and 35, 400%. Transfer patterns to 1" x 12" pine; see "Tracing and Transferring" on page 8.

2. Using jigsaw, cut out angel and wing patterns.

3. Sand edges of wood as necessary.

4. Paint wings with a base coat of yellow. Paint angel with a base coat of blue. Allow to dry.

5. Transfer details of angel and wings; see "Tracing and Transferring" on page 8.

6. Paint details; see pattern and photo for color and placement. Allow to dry.

7. Cut one end of the 6-foot length of 1" x 2" at a diagonal to form the stake; see diagram.

DIAGRAM

8. Antique angel, wings, and stake; see "Antiquing" on page 10.

9. Attach wings to angel back with screws. Attach blunt end of the stake to back of wings and angel, using enough wood screws to hold securely.

10. Seal with exterior varnish.

Every garden needs a Gar"D"en angel. Her benevolent spirit will smile down gently on your favorite flowers or vegetables. Place her anywhere in the ground or attach her directly to the garden gate or wall.

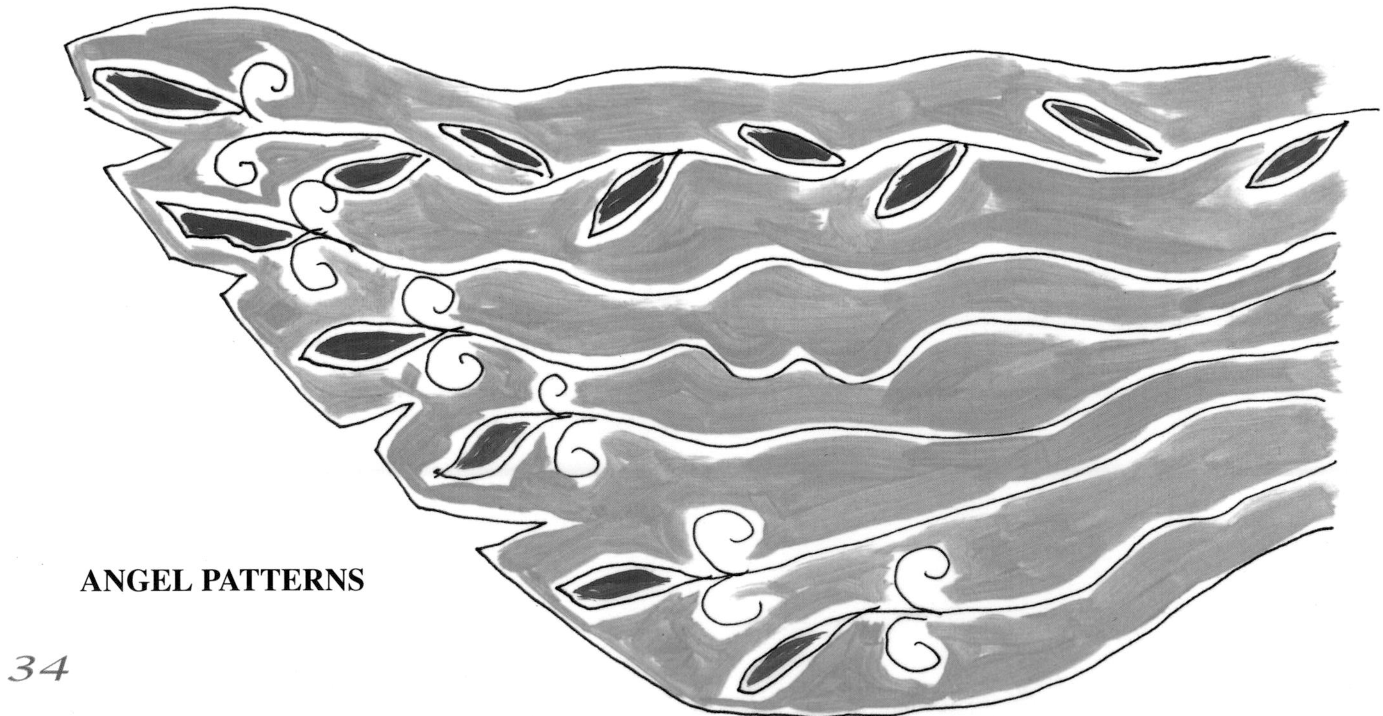

ANGEL PATTERNS

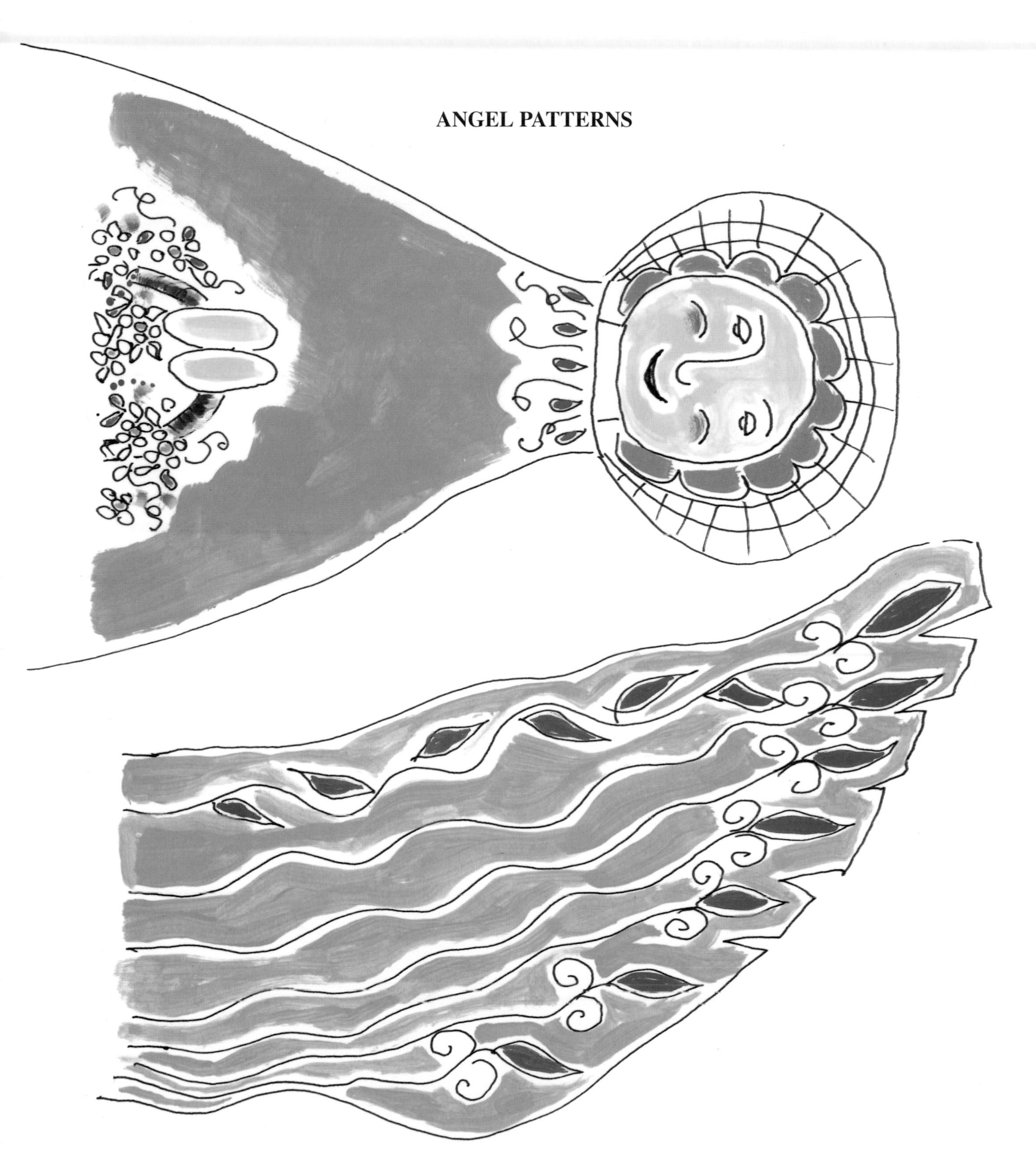
ANGEL PATTERNS

Easter Eggs

Materials

One 1" x 12" piece of pine wood, $2^1/_2$ feet long
Purple, yellow, blue, and white acrylic paint
Three $^5/_{16}$"-diameter wooden dowels, 2 feet to $2^1/_2$ feet long
Glue
Burnt umber artist's oil color
Paint thinner
Oil-based varnish
Exterior varnish

Tools

Photocopy machine
Tracing paper
Transfer paper
Pencil
Jigsaw
Wood clamps
Sandpaper
Drill with $^1/_4$" drill bit
2" utility paintbrush
$^1/_4$" flat artist's brush
#2 round artist's liner brush
Hammer
Rags
Bowl or other small container to mix paint

Directions

1. Using a photocopy machine, enlarge Easter egg patterns, found on pages 38 and 39, 200%. Transfer pattern to 1" x 12" pine; see "Tracing and Transferring" on page 8.

2. Cut out Easter eggs; see "Woodworking" on page 9.

3. Sand edges of wood as necessary.

4. Drill a $^1/_4$" hole in the bottom of each Easter egg.

5. Paint Easter eggs with a base coat of yellow, blue, or purple. Allow to dry.

6. Trace and transfer details for each Easter egg; see "Tracing and Transferring" on page 8.

7. Paint details white on each Easter egg. Allow to dry.

8. Cut dowels to assorted lengths, ranging from 2 feet to $2^1/_2$ feet.

9. Put a dab of glue in each drilled hole and insert a dowel. Hammer in place if necessary.

10. Antique eggs; see "Antiquing" on page 10.

11. Seal with exterior varnish.

Easter eggs are a universal sign of spring. These eggs are decorated with designs inspired by the geometric designs of the elaborate eggs of the Ukraine and other eastern European cultures.

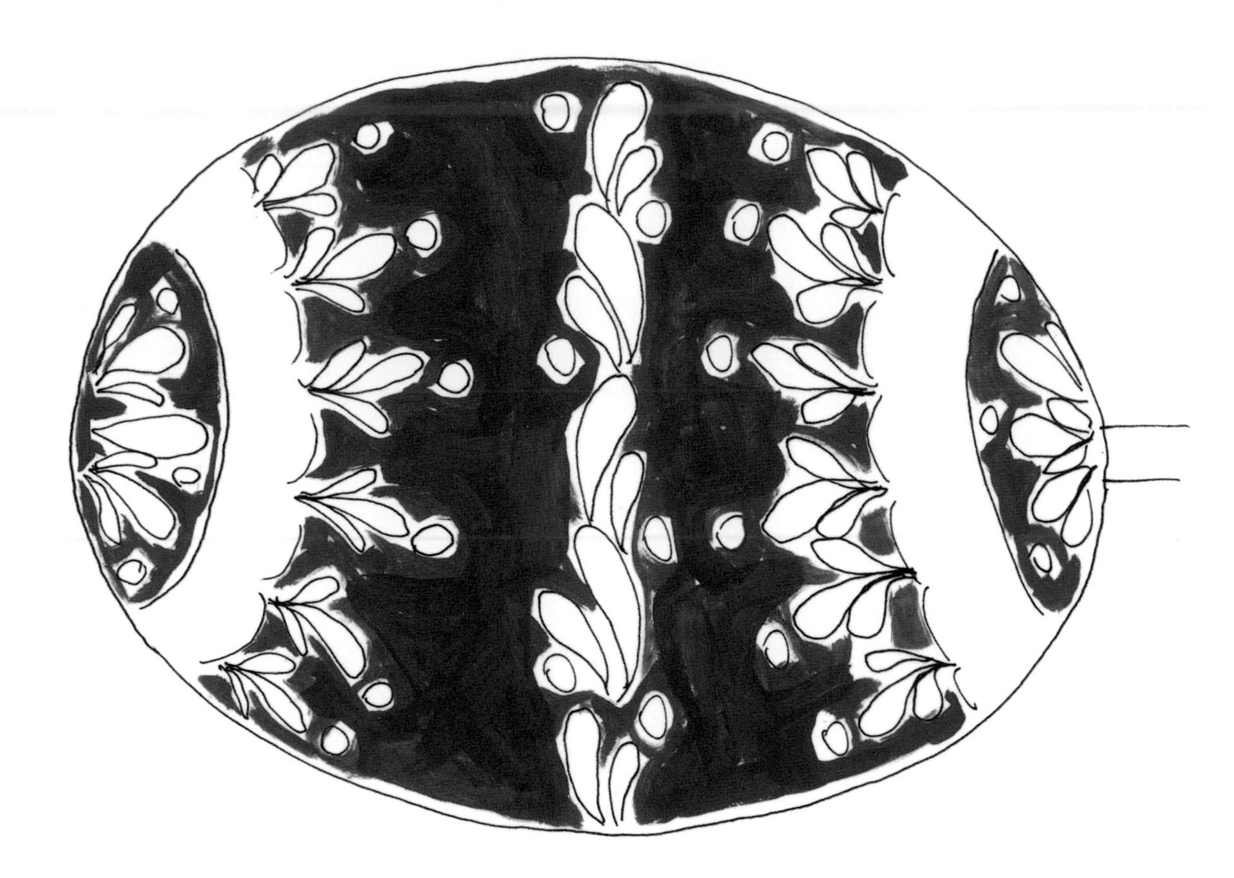

EASTER EGG PATTERNS

EASTER EGG PATTERNS

FLEURS

Fleurs Planter Box

Materials

One 1" x 12" piece of pine wood, 5 feet long
Twelve $1^1/_4$" wood screws
Wood putty
Turquoise, white, dark green, mauve, red, and yellow acrylic paint
Burnt umber artist's oil paint
Paint thinner
Oil-based varnish
Four 4" terra-cotta pots

Tools

Tracing paper
Transfer paper
Table saw
Compass or round object to use as a pattern
Pencil
Jigsaw
Drill with $^1/_2$" drill bit
Countersink bit
Phillips screwdriver or Phillips screwdriver bit
Putty knife
Sandpaper
2" utility paintbrush
$^1/_4$" flat artist's brush
#2 round liner artist's brush

Directions

1. Using a table saw, cut pine into three 24" x $5^1/_2$" pieces for top and sides. Cut two pieces $4^3/_4$" x $5^1/_2$" for opposite sides.

2. On center top of box, mark, drill, and cut four 6" circles; see diagram. Refer to "Woodworking" on page 9.

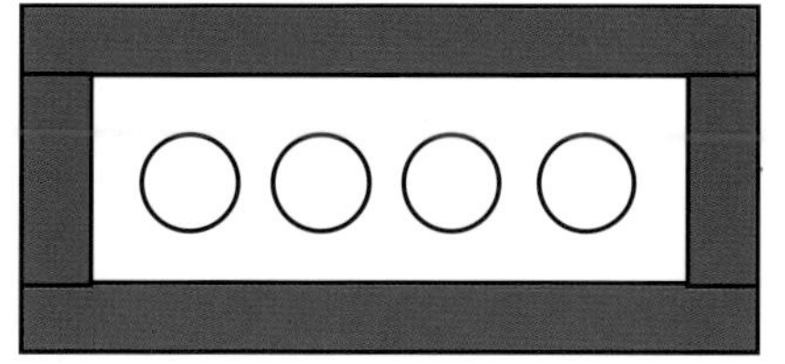

DIAGRAM

3. Assemble box with three countersunk wood screws on each side.

4. Paint box with a base coat of turquoise. Allow to dry.

5. Putty holes. Allow to dry. Sand if necessary.

6. Trace and transfer pattern for "Fleurs" and flowers found on page 42; see "Tracing and Transferring" on page 8.

7. Paint box; see pattern and photo for colors and placement. Allow to dry.

8. Antique box; see "Antiquing" on page 10.

9. Place terra-cotta pots in holes in box.

This beautiful planter says "Fleurs" which is French for flowers.

FLEURS PATTERNS

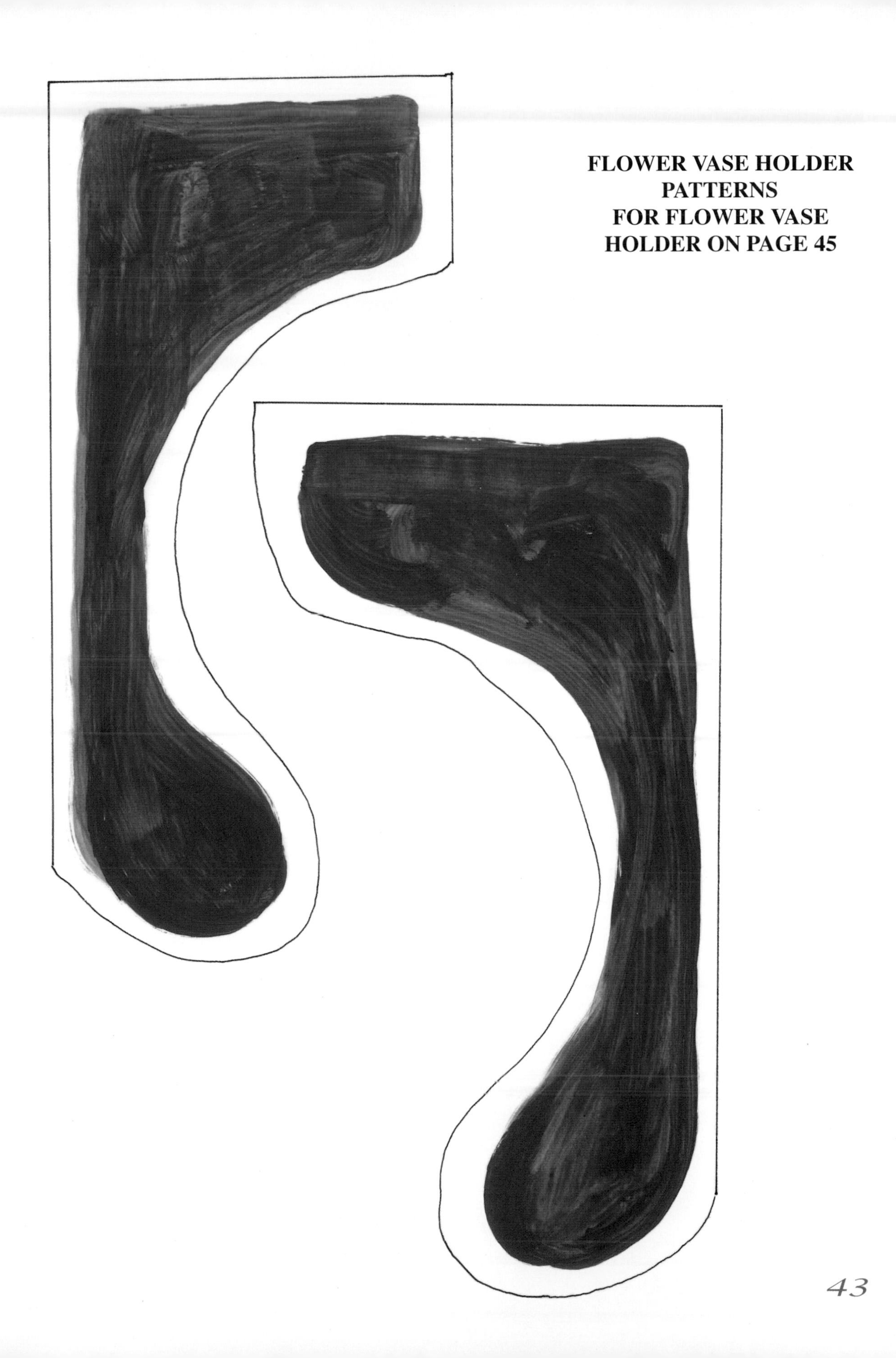

FLOWER VASE HOLDER PATTERNS FOR FLOWER VASE HOLDER ON PAGE 45

Flower Vase Holder

Materials

One 1" x 12" piece of redwood or cedar, 1 foot long
Redwood exterior wood stain
Four 1 1/4" wood screws
5 1/2"-diameter vase or pot
Wood putty

Tools

Tracing paper
Transfer paper
Pencil
Jigsaw
Wood clamps
Sandpaper
Drill with #2 Phillips screw-driver bit
Countersink bit
Putty knife
2" utility paintbrush

Directions

1. Trace and transfer bracket pattern, found on page 43, to 1" x 12" redwood; see "Tracing and Transferring" on page 8.

2. Cut out two brackets; see "Woodworking" on page 9.

3. Attach one bracket to the arm of a chair with two wood screws, countersinking holes.

4. Set the vase or pot in the bracket. Set the other bracket flush with the vase and mark it's position. Remove the vase and screw the second bracket in places as in the previous step.

5. Putty holes, allow to dry. Sand if necessary.

6. Stain brackets with exterior stain. Allow to dry.

7. Place vase in bracket.

This simple bracket attaches a vase of flowers to an ordinary chair. Try it on tables or porch rails too. A terra cotta pot will fit in the brackets as well.

Bench

Materials

Two 2" x 6" pieces of redwood, 8 feet long
One 4" x 6" piece of redwood, 6 feet long
Twenty-two 4"-long wood screws
Wood putty
One 1-quart can of outdoor wood stain

Tools

Table saw or circular saw
Drill with countersink bit
Carpenter's level
Phillips screwdriver
Putty knife
Sandpaper
Shovel
Concrete mix (optional)

Directions

1. Cut 2" x 6" pieces of redwood into three 4-foot lengths for seat pieces, and two $16^1/_2$" lengths for seat supports. Cut the 4" x 6" piece of redwood into two 3-foot lengths for legs.

2. Cut the seat support pieces as in Diagram A.

3. Lay the three seat pieces lengthwise, side by side; see Diagram B. Place the seat supports 2" from outside ends of the seat pieces; see Diagram B. Attach seat supports to seat pieces with twelve screws. As always, be sure to countersink the screws and use a good wood putty to cover the screw holes. Allow to dry; then sand the wood putty flat.

4. Attach one leg to each seat support, using five 4" screws each; see Diagram B.

5. Finish the bench with an all-weather outdoor stain.

6. To place bench, dig two 19"-deep holes in the ground, the same distance apart and slightly larger around as the legs of the bench.

7. Place the legs of the bench in the holes. Using a carpenter's level, make sure the bench is level. Fill the hole with dirt; for added strength and durability, you may choose to fill the holes with a concrete mix.

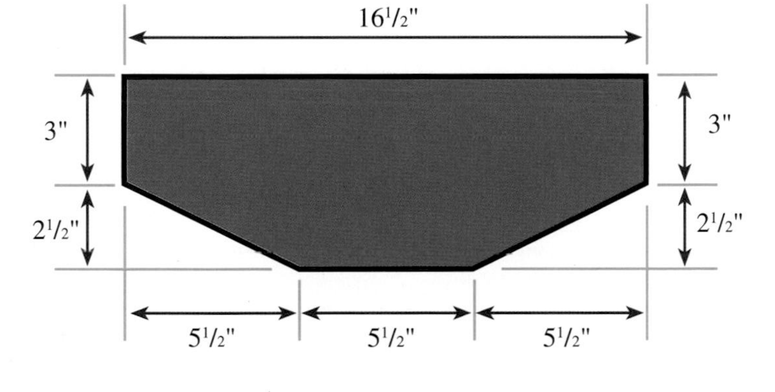

DIAGRAM A

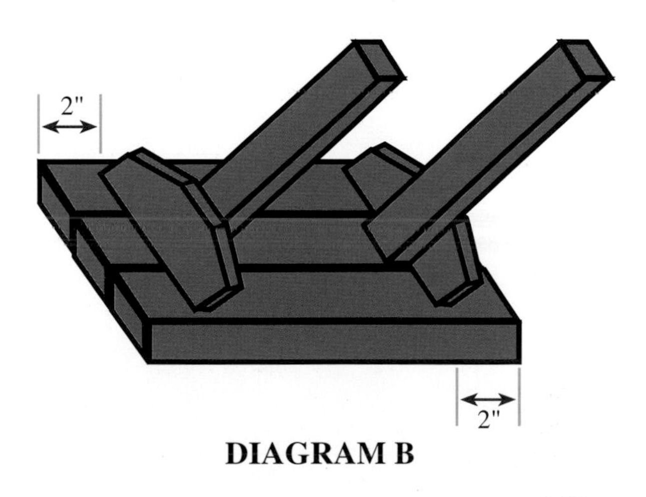

DIAGRAM B

Chapter Two

Summer

Strawberry Box

Materials

One 1" x 12" piece of pine wood, 5 feet long
Twelve $1^{1}/_{4}$" wood screws
Wood putty
Four 4" terra-cotta pots
Turquoise, dark green, red, and yellow acrylic paint
Burnt umber artist's oil paint
Paint thinner
Oil-based varnish
Strawberry wood cutouts
Wood glue
Exterior varnish

Tools

Table saw
Compass or round object to use as a pattern
Pencil
Jigsaw
Drill with $^{1}/_{2}$" drill bit
Countersink
Phillips screwdriver or Phillips screwdriver bit
Putty knife
Sandpaper
2" utility paintbrush
$^{1}/_{4}$" flat artist's brush
#2 round liner artist's brush

Directions

1. Using a table saw, cut pine into three 24" x $5^{1}/_{2}$" pieces for box top, front, and back. Cut two pieces $4^{3}/_{4}$" x $5^{1}/_{2}$" for sides.

2. On center top of box, mark, drill, and cut four 6" circles; see diagram. Refer to "Woodworking" on page 9.

3. Lay out the pieces of the box as shown in the diagram. Attach the longer sides to the shorter sides with two wood screws at each joint. Be sure to predrill the screw hole locations with your countersink bit.

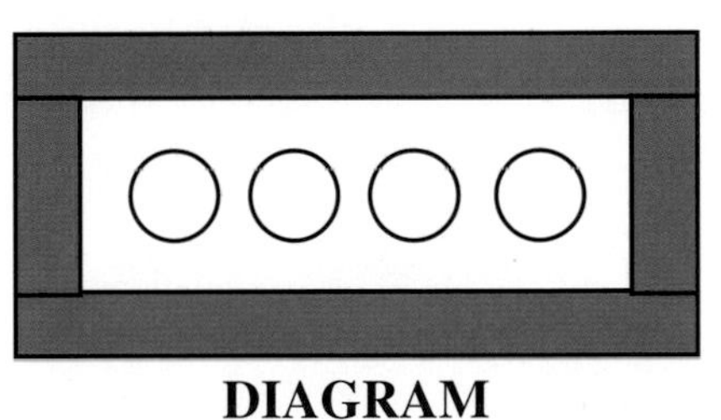

DIAGRAM

4. Attach the top to the box with four countersunk screws running through each side of the box.

5. Putty and sand all countersunk screw locations.

6. Paint box with a base coat of turquoise. Allow to dry.

7. Paint strawberry wood cutouts red; see pattern and photo for colors and placement. Allow to dry.

8. Paint strawberry seeds yellow.

9. Antique box and cutouts; see "Antiquing" on page 10. Allow to dry.

10. Glue cutouts to box.

11. Seal with exterior varnish.

If you would like to cut your own strawberry wood cutouts, a pattern is provided on the following page.

STRAWBERRY PATTERN

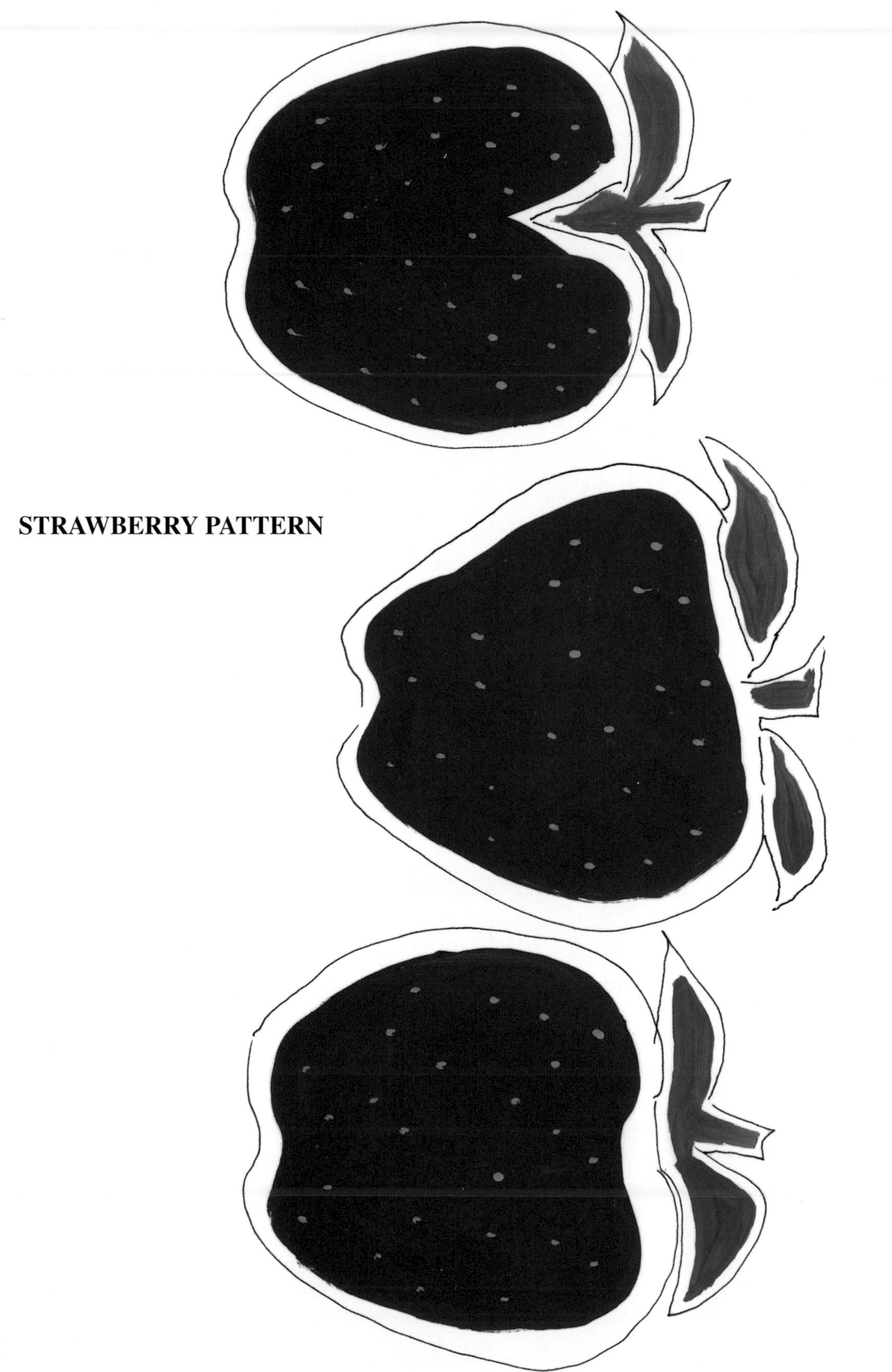

FLAMINGO PATTERN FOR FLAMINGOS ON PAGE 55

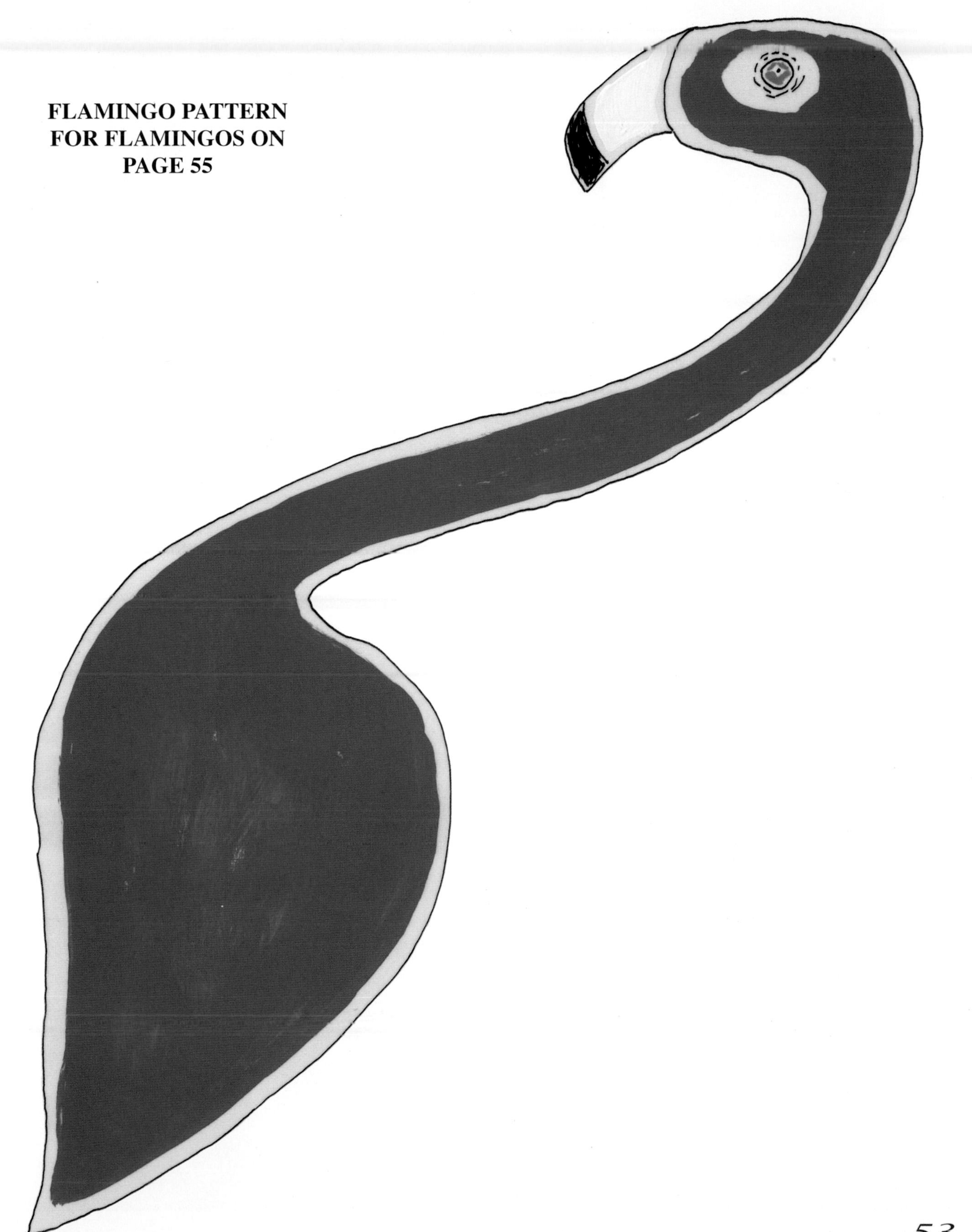

Flamingos

Materials

One 1" x 12" piece of pine, 8 feet long
Three 3/8"-diameter wooden dowels, 3-feet long
Coral, yellow, white, and black acrylic paint
Burnt umber artist's oil paint
Paint thinner
Varnish
Exterior varnish
Wood glue

Tools

Photocopy machine
Tracing paper
Transfer paper
Pencil
Jigsaw
Drill with 7/16" bit
2"-wide utility paintbrush
1/4" flat artist's paintbrush
#2 round artist's liner brush
Hammer
Rags
Small container to mix paint

Directions

1. Using a photocopy machine, enlarge flamingo pattern, found on page 53, 200%. Transfer enlarged pattern to 1" x 12" pine; see "Tracing and Transferring" on page 8.

2. Using jigsaw, cut out flamingo; see "Woodworking" on page 9. Using cutout as a pattern, cut two more flamingos.

3. Paint flamingos with a base coat of coral. Allow to dry.

4. Transfer details to painted flamingo; see "Tracing and Transferring" on page 8.

5. Paint details. Allow to dry.

6. Using drill, drill a hole in the bottom of each flamingo.

7. Put a dab of wood glue in each hole and insert dowels. Hammer in place if necessary.

8. Antique flamingos; see "Antiquing" on page 10.

9. Seal with exterior varnish.

Although flamingos are naturally found in warm, wetland areas, they are often seen as lawn ornaments everywhere. Their exotic look, graceful necks, and unusual coloring causes many to find them fascinating.

Le Jardin

Le Jardin Plaque

Materials

One 1" x 12" piece of pine wood, 2 feet long
One 1" x 2" piece of pine wood, 6 feet long
Blue, white, peach, red, dark green, tan, yellow, orange, light blue, and brown acrylic paint
Burnt umber artist's oil color
Paint thinner
Oil-based varnish
Exterior varnish
Three $1^1/_4$" wood screws

Tools

Photocopy machine
Tracing paper
Transfer paper
Pencil
Jigsaw
Wood clamps
Sandpaper
Ruler or straightedge
Drill with #2 Phillips screw-driver bit
Bowl or other small container to mix paint
Rags
1" flat artist's brush
$^1/_4$" flat artist's brush
#2 round liner artist's brush

Directions

1. Using a photocopy machine, enlarge plaque pattern, found on page 58, 200%. Transfer patterns to 1" x 12" pine; see "Tracing and Transferring" on page 8.

2. Using jigsaw, cut out plaque.

3. Sand edges of wood as necessary.

4. Paint plaque with a base coat of blue.

5. Transfer details to plaque; see "Tracing and Transferring" on page 8.

6. Paint details; see pattern and photo for color and placement. Allow to dry.

7. Cut one end of the 6-foot length of 1" x 2" pine at a diagonal to form the stake; see diagram.

DIAGRAM

8. Antique plaque and stake; see "Antiquing" on page 10.

9. Attach wide end of the stake to back of the plaque with wood screws.

10. Seal with exterior varnish.

This garden sign has an old-fashioned European look that is reminiscent of garden signs in the Provence area of France. Le jardin is French for garden. This pretty basket overflowing with garden flowers will give a touch of old-world charm to any garden.

Le Jardin

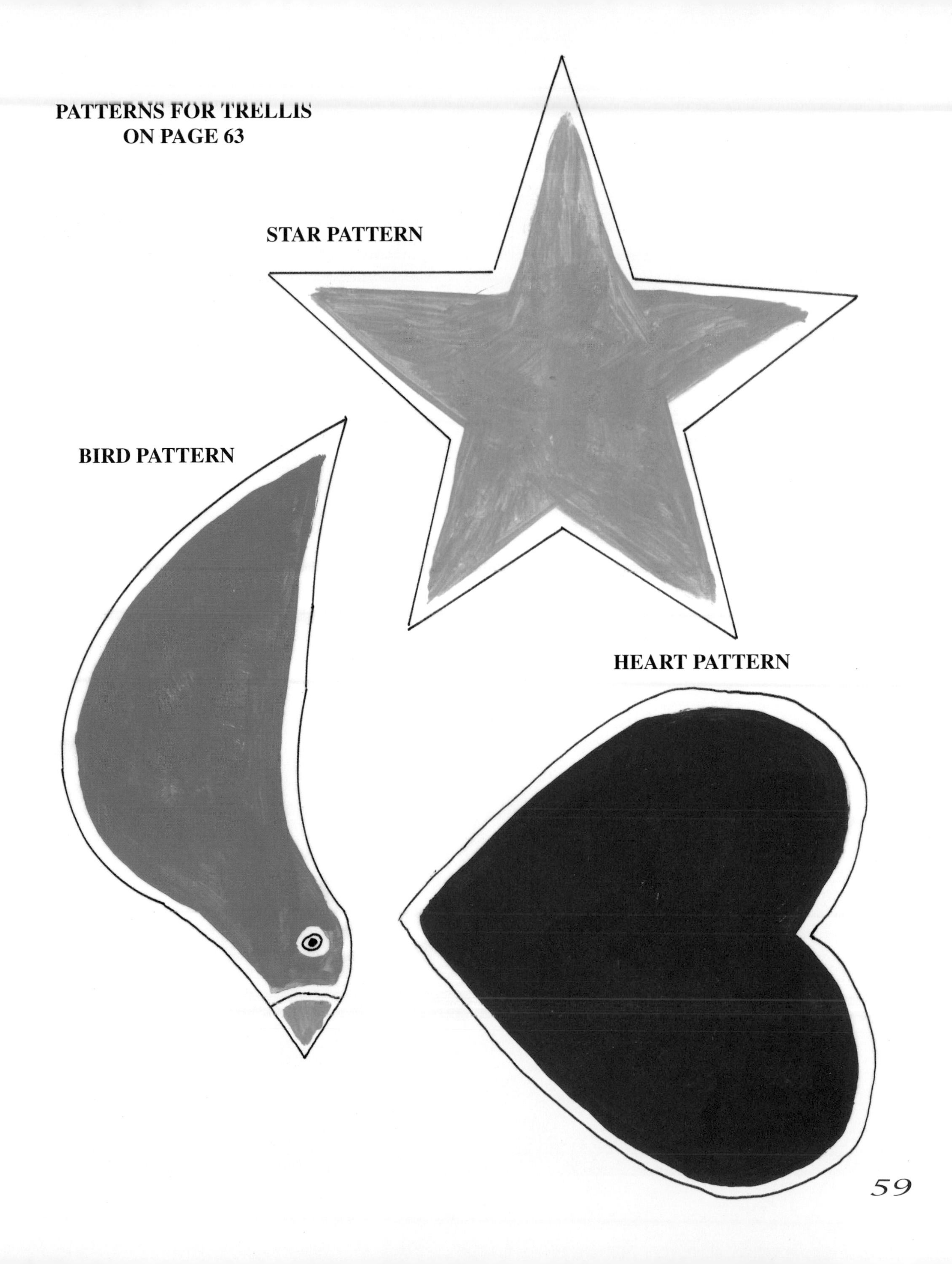
PATTERNS FOR TRELLIS
ON PAGE 63
STAR PATTERN
BIRD PATTERN
HEART PATTERN

Garden Trellis

Materials

One 1" x 12" piece of pine wood, $1^1/_2$ feet long
Red, yellow, and blue acrylic paint
Burnt umber artist's paint
Paint thinner
Oil-based varnish
Exterior varnish
One white trellis
Wood glue

Tools

Tracing paper
Transfer paper
Pencil
Jigsaw
Wood clamps
Sandpaper
2" utility paintbrush
1" flat artist's brush

Directions

1. Trace and transfer patterns on page 59 to 1" x 12" pine; see "Tracing and Transferring" on page 8.

2. Cut out one heart, one star, and one bird; see "Woodworking" on page 9.

3. Using cutouts as patterns, mark and cut out three more hearts, three more stars, and one more bird.

4. Sand edges of wood as necessary.

5. Paint hearts red, stars yellow, and birds blue. Reverse one bird so that they face each other.

6. Antique hearts, stars, and birds; see "Antiquing" on page 10.

7. Glue hearts, stars, and birds to trellis; see photo for placement. Allow to dry.

8. Seal with exterior varnish.

A plain ordinary trellis can be found in any garden shop. With a little imagination, they can be transformed into extraordinary accents for your yard.

Fountain

Materials

One piece of $^{3}/_{4}$" diameter PVC pipe, 4 feet long
Two 90-degree PVC elbows
One PVC adaptor to faucet
One 25" diameter galvanized metal tub
One 15" diameter galvanized metal tub
One 1 gallon galvanized metal watering can
One decorative copper faucet with verdigris finish
One standard swamp cooler pump
One piece of $^{1}/_{4}$" diameter water line, 6 feet long
One piece of $^{1}/_{2}$" diameter electrical conduit, 4 feet long
Copper wire
One conduit bracket (U strap)
Two self-tapping screws
PVC primer and glue
Silicone
Exterior primer
Red, green, white, and black acrylic paints
Metal primer
Potting soil
Plants

Tools

Drill with 1" drill bit
Tracing paper
Transfer paper
2" utility paintbrush
1" flat artist's brush
$^{1}/_{4}$" flat artist's brush

Directions

1. Place smaller tub inside larger tub. Drill a 1" hole through both tubs, approximately 2" from tub bottom.

2. Run waterline through electrical conduit, leaving equal excess at both ends.

3. Cut a 3-foot length of $^{3}/_{4}$" PVC pipe. Run waterline/ electrical conduit through $^{3}/_{4}$" PVC pipe.

4. Connect 90-degree elbows on both ends of 3-foot length of $^{3}/_{4}$" PVC pipe, sealing all joints with PVC primer and gluing according to manufacturer's instructions.

5. On bottom end of 3-foot length of $^{3}/_{4}$" PVC pipe, connect remaining 1-foot length of $^{3}/_{4}$" PVC pipe, being careful of electrical wire.

6. On top end of 3-foot length of $^{3}/_{4}$" PVC pipe, attach faucet adapter.

7. Put faucet on adapter, feeding $^{1}/_{4}$" waterline through faucet shut-off valve; cut off excess. Leave shut-off valve completely open.

8. Insert 1-foot length of $^{3}/_{4}$" PVC pipe through holes in both tubs, being careful of electrical wire.

9. Place conduit bracket about 2" from top of outer tub to connect $^{3}/_{4}$" PVC pipe.

10. Leave 12" of $^{1}/_{4}$" waterline in inner tub to connect to water pump.

11. Connect waterline to swamp cooler pump.

12. Seal pipe in holes in tubs with silicone. Let dry for twelve hours.

13. Hang watering can from faucet, fastening with copper wire.

14. Position watering can as necessary so that it will pour into inner tub.

15. Fill outer tub with dirt and plant plants.

16. Fill inner tub with water, adjusting water level so that when circulating, water will not flow out the top of the watering can.

17. Paint tubs with metal primer. Paint pipe with exterior primer.

18. Paint tubs and pipe according to patterns and photo.

FOUNTAIN PATTERN
ENLARGE 430%

Tiered Jardiniere

Materials

Three terra-cotta pots, approximately 22", 18", and 12" diameter
28" of 1/2"-diameter #4 reinforcing steel bar (rebar)
Potting soil

Directions

1. Fill largest pot with potting soil, leaving room for plants.

2. Place the steel bar in the center of this pot.

3. Place the medium-sized pot on top of the largest pot, sliding the steel bar through the drain hole at bottom of pot.

4. Fill the medium-sized pot with potting soil.

5. Place the smallest pot on top of the medium-sized pot, sliding the steel bar through the drain hole at the bottom of pot.

6. Fill the small pot with potting soil, covering the steel bar.

The word jardiniere means tired or stacked. A simple idea, yet so elegant. It would be right at home in Napoleon and Josephine's gardens at Versailles.

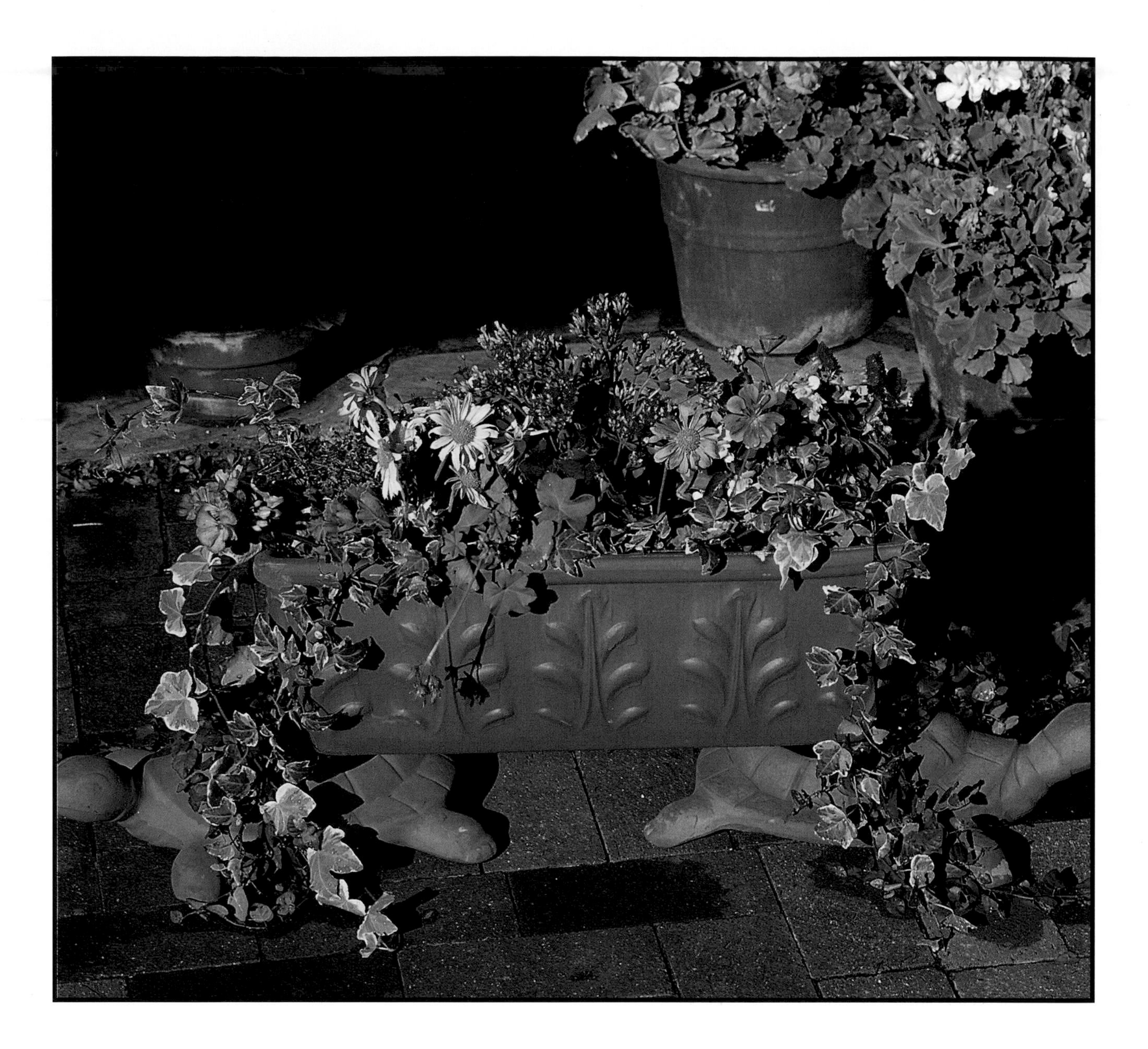

Turtle Planter

Materials

One rectangular terra-cotta pot, approximately 21" x 9"
Two turtle-shaped pots, approximately 16" long
Potting soil

Directions

1. Fill turtle pots with soil.

2. Stack rectangular pot on top of turtle pots.

3. Fill rectangular pot with soil.

4. Fill both pots with plants.

Stacked Floral Pots

Materials

One rectangular terra-cotta pot, approximately 18" x 6"
One square terra-cotta pot, approximately 4" x 4"
Potting soil

Directions

1. Fill rectangular pot with potting soil.

2. Stack square pot on top of rectangular pot.

3. Fill square pot with soil.

4. Fill both pots with plants.

Hanging Sunflower Feeder

Materials

- One 1" x 12" piece of pine wood, $1^1/_2$ feet long
- Yellow and brown acrylic paint
- Three 3" lengths of small chain
- One 8" round cake pan
- Three $^1/_2$" cup hooks
- One 1-foot length of 16-gauge tie wire
- Exterior varnish

Tools

- Photocopy machine
- Tracing paper
- Transfer paper
- Pencil
- Jigsaw
- Sandpaper
- 1" flat artist's brush
- 2" utility paintbrush

Directions

1. Enlarge sunflower pattern, found on page 69, 200%. Transfer enlarged pattern to 1" x 12" pine; see "Tracing and Transferring" on page 8.

2. Cut out center of sunflower, then cut out sunflower; see "Woodworking" on page 9.

3. Paint sunflower yellow. Paint entire cake pan brown.

4. Place three cup hooks, spaced equal distance apart, on top of sunflower petals.

5. Hang one piece of chain on each hook.

6. Join all chain lengths with tie wire; then hang planter with remaining length.

7. Cake pan sits in the center hole of the sunflower. Seal with exterior varnish.

SUNFLOWER PATTERN
FOR HANGING SUNFLOWER FEEDER AND SUNFLOWER FEEDER

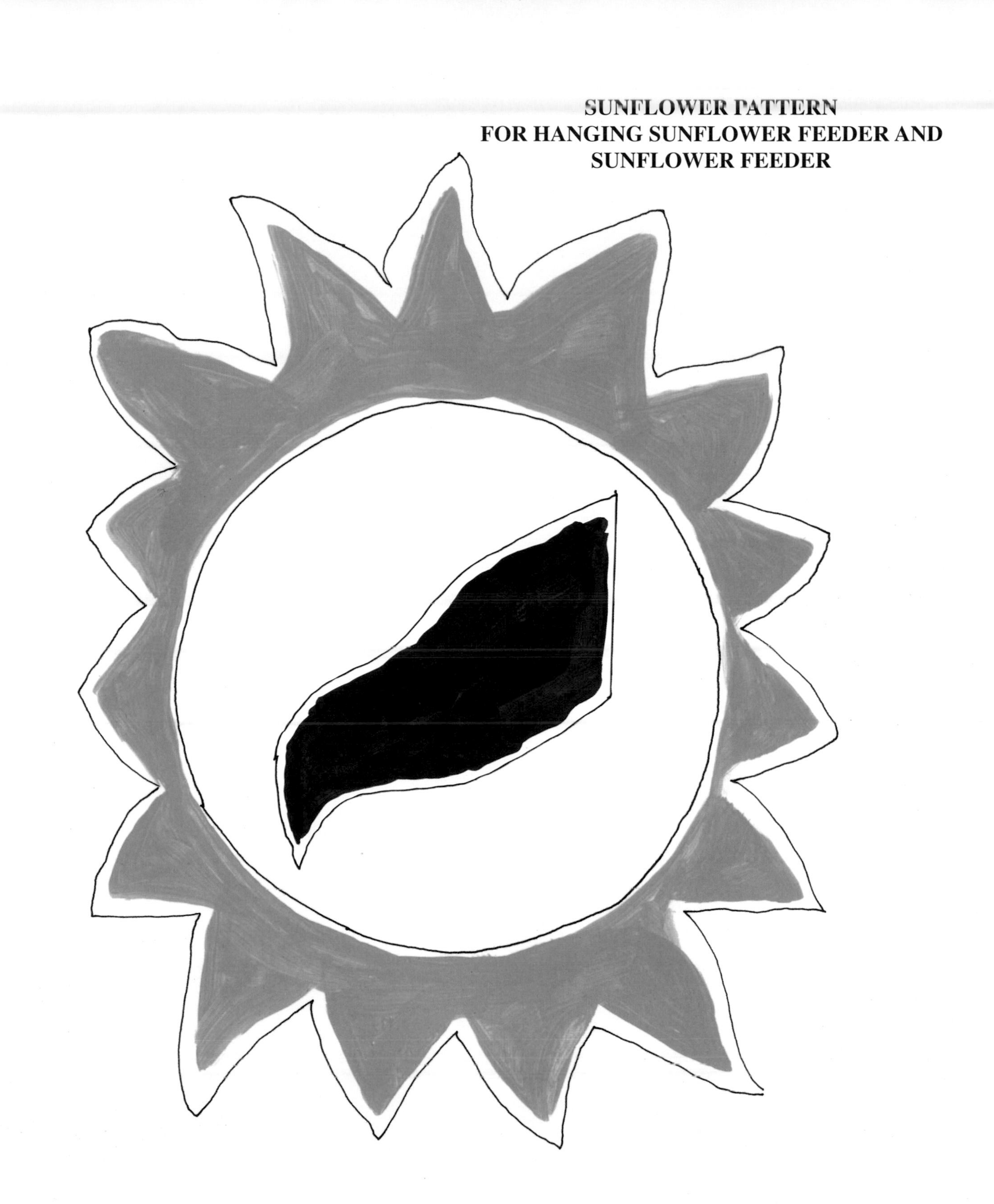

Sunflower Bird Feeder

Materials

One 1" x 12" piece of pine wood, 2 feet long
One 1" x 2" piece of pine wood, 54" long
Yellow, green, and brown acrylic paint
Wood glue
One 8" round cake pan
Three 1$^1/_4$" wood screws
Exterior varnish

Tools

Photocopy machine
Tracing paper
Transfer paper
Pencil
Jigsaw
Wire cutters
Drill with a $^1/_2$" and a $^1/_8$" drill bit
1" flat artist's brush
2" utility paintbrush

Directions

1. Enlarge sunflower and leaf patterns, found on page 69, 200%. Transfer enlarged pattern to 1" x 12" pine; see "Tracing and Transferring" on page 8.

2. Cut out two leaves. Cut out center of sunflower, then cut out sunflower; see "Woodworking" on page 9.

3. Cut one end of the 54" length of 1" x 2" at a diagonal to form the stake; see diagram.

DIAGRAM

4. Paint entire cake pan brown.

5. Paint leaves and the stake green.

6. Paint sunflower yellow.

7. Paint the cake pan brown.

8. Drill a $^1/_8$" hole on stake. Drill $^1/_8$" holes on leaves, $^1/_2$" from edges.

9. Secure leaves to stake with wire.

10. Glue cake pan to center of sunflower.

11. Drill a $^1/_8$" hole on stake. Attach cake pan to stake with wood screw.

12. Seal with exterior varnish.

Garden Markers

Materials

One piece of 1" x 12" pine wood, 5 feet long
One piece of 1" x 8" pine wood, 2 feet long
Ten $1^1/_4$" wood screws
One $1^1/_2$-foot length of 16-gauge tie wire
Glue
Dark green, light green, orange, yellow, red, white, and black acrylic paint
Burnt umber artist's paint
Paint thinner
Oil-based varnish
Exterior varnish

Tools

Photocopy machine
Tracing paper
Transfer paper
Pencil
Table saw with rip fence
Jigsaw
1" flat artist's brush
$^1/_4$" flat artist's brush
#2 round liner artist's brush
2" utility paintbrush
Rags
Bowl or small container to mix paint
Drill with a $^1/_{16}$" drill bit
Phillips screwdriver or drill with Phillips bit

Directions

1. Using a photocopy machine, enlarge marker patterns, found on pages 74, 75, and 76, 200%.

2. Transfer enlarged patterns to 1" x 12" pine; see "Tracing and Transferring" on page 8.

3. Cut out markers; see "Woodworking" on page 9.

4. Paint markers with a base coat; see patterns and photo for color and placement.

5. Trace and transfer details to markers; see "Tracing and Transferring" on page 8.

6. Paint details. Allow to dry.

7. Drill a $^1/_{16}$" hole in top of peas marker. Coil a length of wire around a pencil or other like object. Remove pencil and paint wire green. Glue wire in hole.

8. Using a table saw, cut five 1" x 1" stakes, 2 feet long.

9. Cut one end of each stake at a diagonal; see diagram.

DIAGRAM

10. Attach the back of one marker to the blunt end of each stake with two wood screws.

11. Antique markers and stakes; see "Antiquing" on page 10.

12. Seal with exterior varnish.

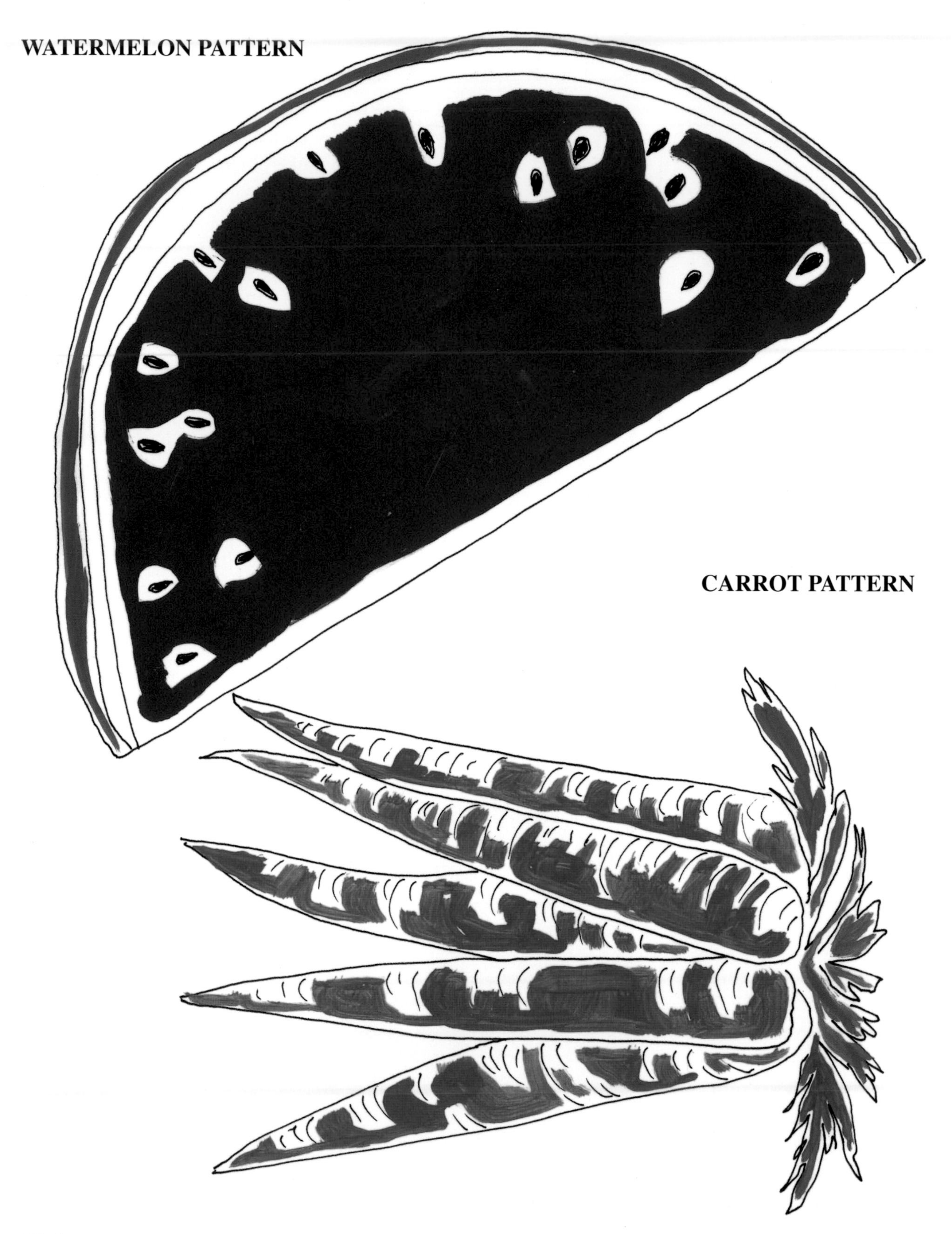
WATERMELON PATTERN
CARROT PATTERN

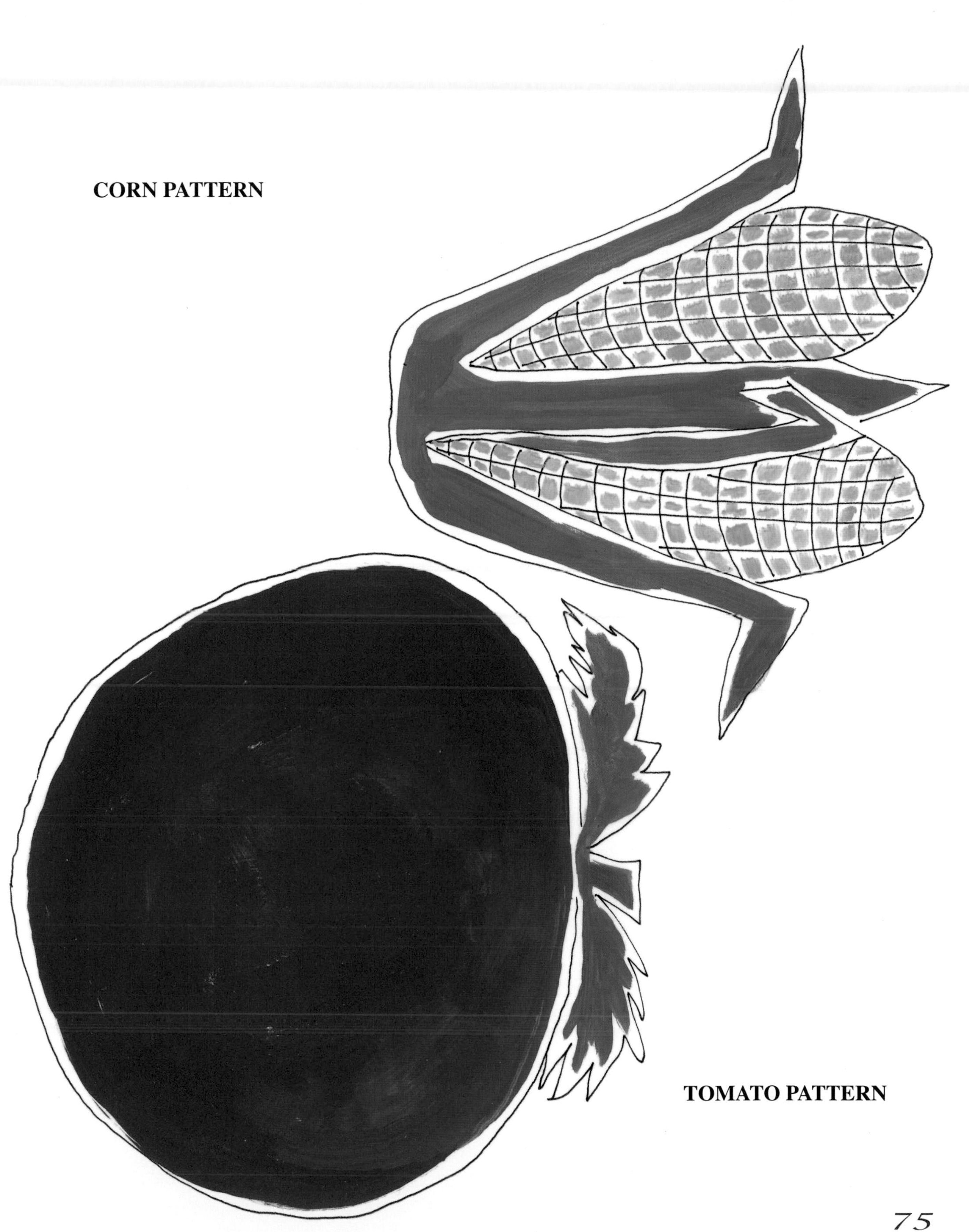
CORN PATTERN
TOMATO PATTERN

PEAS PATTERN

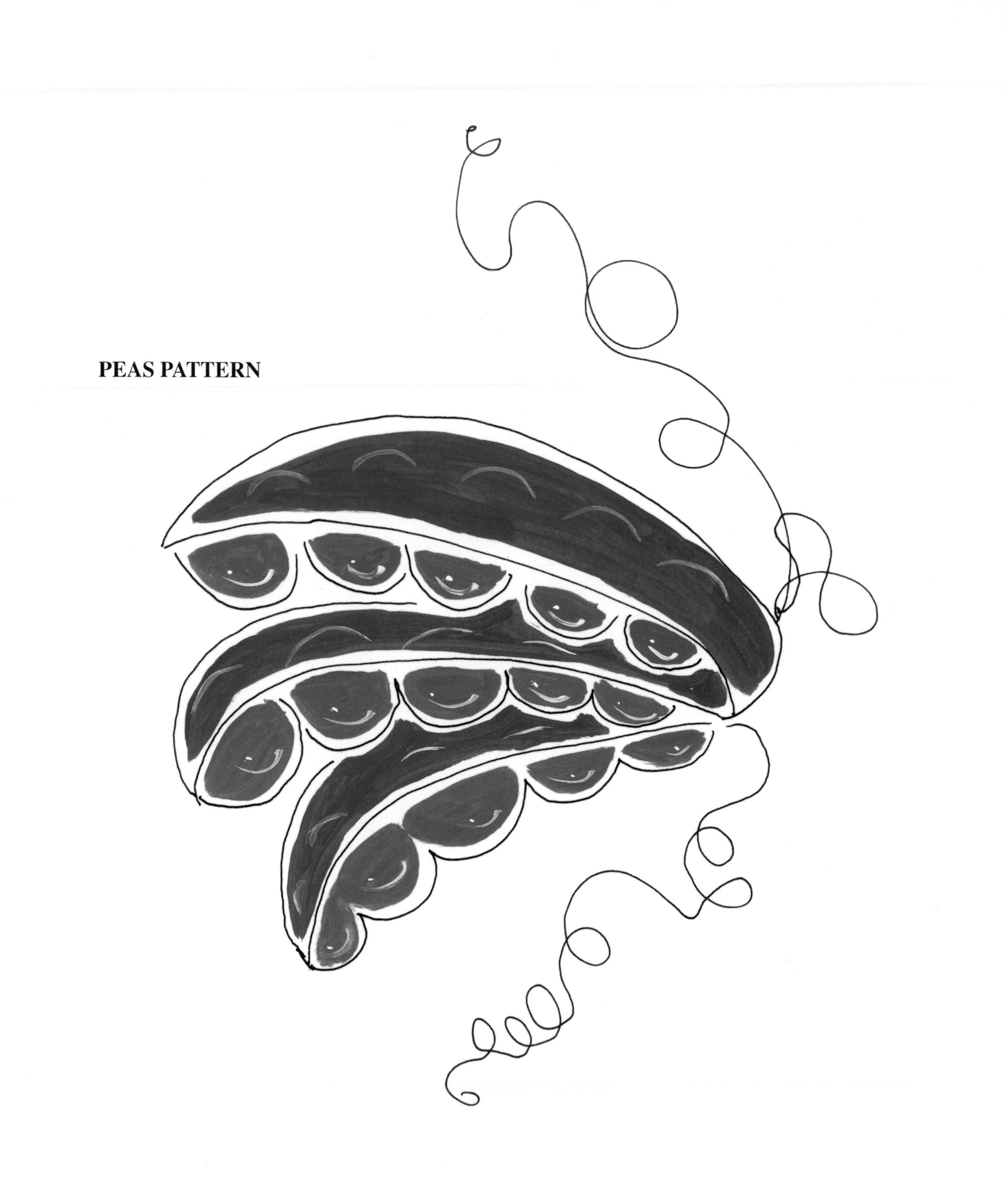

Cow Pot

Materials

One 7" terra-cotta pot
Seven wooden cow cutouts
White, black, and peach acrylic paint

Tools

1/4" flat artist's brush
Hot glue gun and glue sticks

This pot is simple enough for children to complete. Hobby and craft stores carry hundreds of small wood cutouts; you could use just about anything. How about apples for the teacher?

Directions

1. Paint wooden cow cutouts with a base coat of white paint. Allow to dry.

2. Paint cow udders peach. Allow to dry.

3. Paint black spots randomly on cows. Allow to dry.

4. Hot-glue cows to upper edge of pot.

Umbrella Planter

Materials

One 2" x 6" piece of redwood, 5½ feet long
Twenty-four 2¼" wood screws
One piece of 15" x 15" exterior grade plywood, ¾" thick
5" length of 2"-diameter PVC pipe
Clear silicone sealant caulk
Wood putty
Transparent redwood exterior stain
Four ornamental wood cutouts
Wood glue

Tools

Table saw
#2 Phillips screwdriver or drill with #2 Phillips screw bit
Countersink bit
Drill with 2" wood drill bit
Pencil
Sandpaper
2" utility paintbrush

Directions

1. Cut two 15" and two 18" pieces of 2" x 6" redwood for the box.

2. Lay out the pieces of the box as shown in the diagram. Attach the longer sides to the shorter sides with two wood screws at each joint. Be sure to predrill the screw hole locations with your countersink bit.

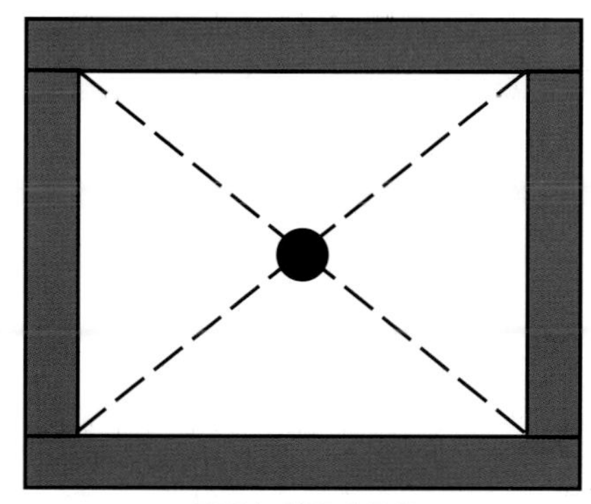

DIAGRAM

3. Drill a 2"-diameter hole in the center of the plywood bottom. To locate the center, draw an "X" from corner to corner. The center will be the intersection of the lines; see diagram.

4. Attach the plywood to the bottom of the box with two countersunk screws running through each side of the box.

5. Putty and sand all countersunk screw locations.

6. Put the PVC pipe over center hole and caulk with sealant. Caulk all interior seams of the box.

7. Stain the box and wood cutouts with transparent redwood stain; allow to dry.

8. Glue wood cutouts to sides of box.

This planter box will enhance any patio and table, and is deep enough and big enough to hold bunches of flowers. The umbrella post is protected by the pipe in the center of the planter.

Patio Umbrella Table

Materials

Nine pieces of 2" x 4" redwood, 8 feet long
Four pieces of 2" x 4" redwood, 10 feet long
Four pieces of 2" x 4" redwood, 6 feet long
110 (3") wood screws
Eight pieces of 2" x 4" redwood, $58^1/_2$" long
Four pieces of 2" x 4" redwood, 28" long
Wood putty, redwood color
Semi-transparent exterior stain, redwood color

Tools

Table saw
Drill with #2 Phillips screw-driver bit
Countersink bit
Putty knife
Sandpaper
4" utility paintbrush
Rags
Drop cloth

Directions

1. From 8-foot long 2" x 4" redwood pieces, cut thirteen 45"-long pieces for the table top surface, cut two 45"-long pieces for the table top frame, and cut two 48"-long pieces for the table top frame.

2. From 10-foot long 2" x 4" redwood pieces, cut eight $58^1/_2$"-long pieces for the table base.

3. From 6-foot long 2" x 4" redwood pieces, cut four 28"-long pieces for the legs.

4. Using drill with countersink bit, lay out and predrill the two 48"-long frame pieces as shown in Diagram A.

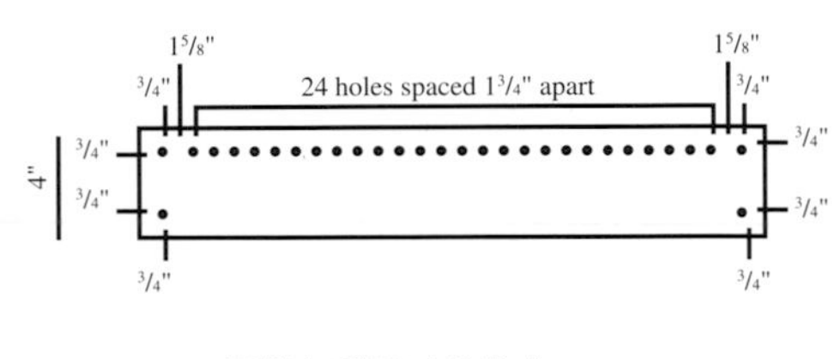

DIAGRAM A

5. Attach the thirteen redwood pieces to the two 48" frame pieces with wood screws, utilizing the predrilled holes.

6. Attach the two 48" frame pieces with wood screws.

7. Cut each of the eight base pieces as shown in Diagram B. This is the most difficult part of the project. When completed, the pieces will fit together as

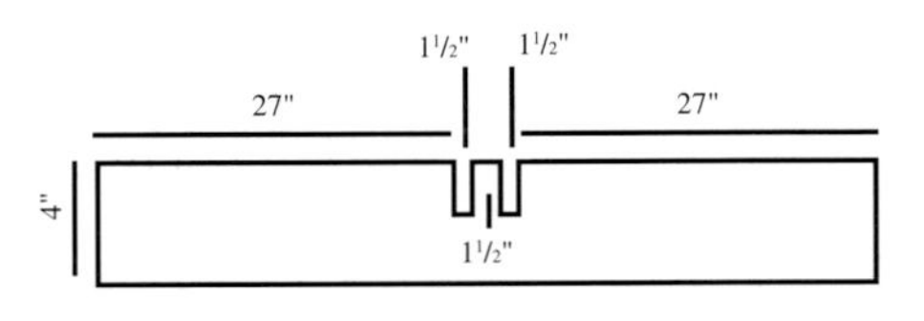

DIAGRAM B

shown in Diagram C. You may want to practice this using two scarp pieces of wood before making the real cuts. Be sure to set the depth of your cut exactly ½ the width of your 2" x 4" so the pieces will fit together perfectly.

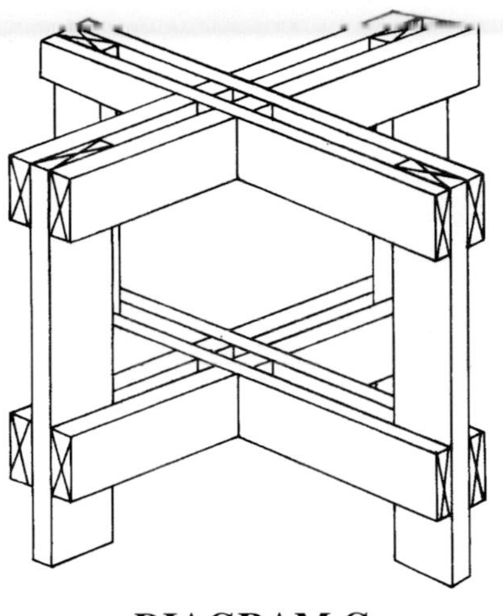

DIAGRAM C

8. After cutting the eight 58½"-long redwood pieces, assemble two sets of cross pieces; see Diagram D.

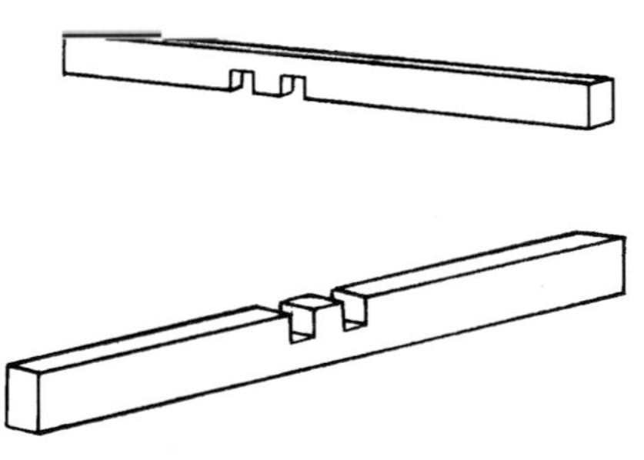

DIAGRAM D

9. Assemble the base as shown

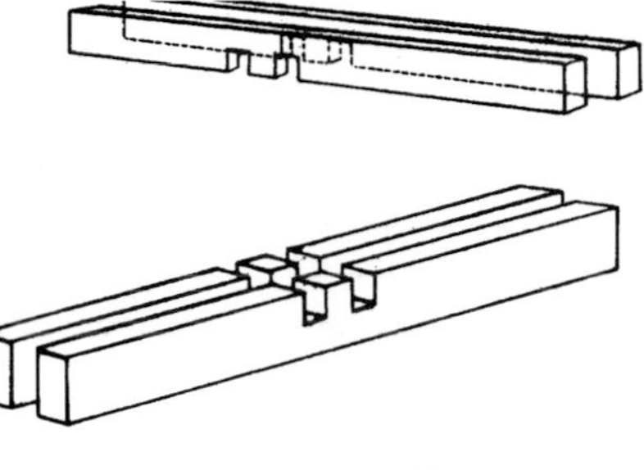

DIAGRAM E

in Diagram E. Attach four leg pieces sandwiched between interlocked cross pieces. Attach at the top and 4" up from bottom. Do not have the lower cross pieces resting on the ground.

10. Set top on base.

11. Putty all countersunk holes. Allow to dry.

12. Sand putty smooth.

3. Stain table following manufacturer's instructions. Allow to dry.

Porch Swing Stand

Materials

Four 2" x 4" pieces of redwood, 10 feet long
Two 2" x 4" pieces of redwood, 6 feet long
Two 2" x 4" pieces of redwood, $2^1/_2$ feet long
One 4" x 4" piece of redwood, 10 feet long
Two 4" x 4" pieces of redwood, 8 feet long
Four 2" x 4" pieces of redwood, 5 feet long
Sixteen $2^1/_2$" flat-head wood screws
Twenty-eight 4" flat-head wood screws
Four eye hooks
Four eyebolts

Tools

Table saw or circular saw
Pencil
Wood chisel
Hammer
Sandpaper
Phillips screwdriver or drill with phillips screw bit
Drill and countersink bit
Carpenter's level

Directions

1. Lay out two of the 10-foot pieces of 2" x 4" redwood according to the diagram. Mark both pieces where they cross each other at Joint X for notching.

2. To notch the area where both pieces cross, set the saw blade to half the width of the wood and make several cuts between the marks. Remove remaining wood with a chisel and hammer.

3. Lay both pieces out again, interlocking them at Joint X to form legs.

4. Lay the 6-foot piece of 2" x 4" redwood across legs. Attach with wood screws.

5. Attach the 8-foot piece of 4" x 4" redwood vertically to legs at Joint X with wood screws; see Diagram.

6. Lay out the $2^1/_2$-foot piece of 2" x 4" redwood at the top of the legs; see Diagram. Mark the placement of the top edge. Cut the legs so that they lie flush with the $2^1/_2$-foot redwood piece. Cut the bottom of the legs so that they will rest flat on the floor. Attach the $2^1/_2$-foot redwood piece to legs with wood screws.

7. Repeat Steps 1–6 to make two more legs.

8. Place the 10-foot piece of 4" x 4" redwood between the two sets of legs for the top beam. Attach with wood screws.

9. Stand the swing support upright and mark the placement of the four 5-foot pieces of 2" x 4" redwood; see photo for placement. Cut each piece and attach to support with 4" screws, using a carpenter's level to ensure each piece is level.

10. Attach the eye hooks to hang flowerpots on. Attach the eyebolts to hang the swing.

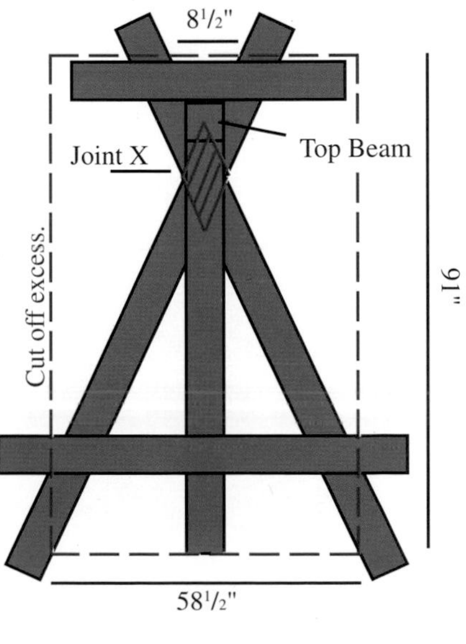

DIAGRAM

Garden Hose Box

Materials

Four 2" x 10" pieces of redwood, 3 feet long
Ten 4"-wide pieces of cedar fencing, 3 feet long
Two 2" x 4" pieces of redwood, $29^1/_2$" long
Two 2" x 4" pieces of redwood, 36" long
One 3-foot square piece of $^1/_2$" CDX exterior grade plywood
One 1" x 12" piece of pine wood, 1 foot long
Fifty $1^1/_2$" wood screws
Twenty $2^1/_2$" wood screws
Two 4" hinges
Black, red, white, yellow, green, and blue acrylic paint
Cape Cod gray semi-transparent exterior stain
Exterior varnish

Directions

1. Lay out the pieces of the box as shown in the diagram. Attach the 2" x 10" pieces of redwood together with two wood screws at each joint to form sides. Be sure to predrill the screw hole locations with your countersink bit.

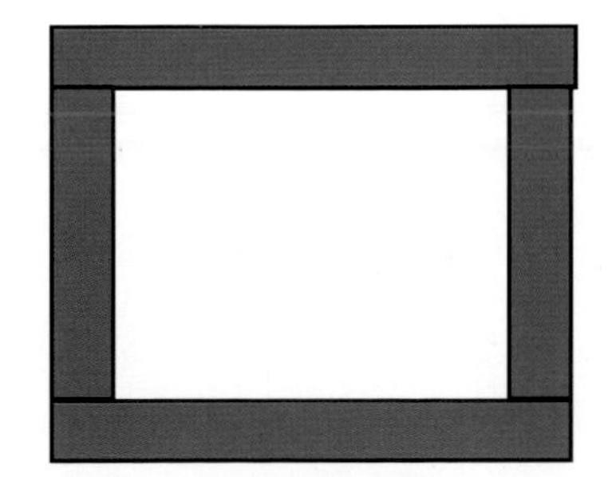

DIAGRAM

Tools

Table saw
Phillips screwdriver or drill with Phillips bit
Drill with $^1/_2$" drill bit and $1^1/_2$" drill bit
Tracing paper
Transfer paper
Pencil
Jigsaw
Sandpaper
3" utility paintbrush
$^1/_4$" flat artist's brush
#2 round liner artist's brush

2. Attach the two 36" long pieces of 2" x 4" redwood to plywood to form legs and base; see photo.

3. Attach the legs and base to the bottom of the box with two countersunk screws running through each side of the box.

4. Attach two of the cedar fence pieces, tightly butted against each other, on the back opening of box.

5. To make lid, attach the eight remaining cedar fence pieces, spaced $^1/_2$" apart between the two $29^1/_2$"-long pieces of 2" x 4" redwood with wood screws.

6. Set the lid on the back opening of the box beside the two cedar fence pieces. Attach lid to cedar fence pieces with hinges.

7. Drill several $^1/_2$" holes in plywood base to allow water to drain.

8. Drill a $1^1/_2$" hole in the back or side of the box to thread hose through.

9. Stain box with exterior stain.

10. Trace and transfer heart pattern, found on page 86, to the 1" x 12" piece of pine; see "Tracing and Transferring" on page 8.

11. Cut out heart; see "Woodworking" on page 9.

12. Paint heart with a base coat of black paint. Allow to dry.

13. Trace and transfer details of heart.

14. Paint details, referring to pattern and photo for color and placement.

15. Seal with exterior varnish.

16. Attach heart to front side of box with wood screws.

HEART PATTERN

PATTERNS FOR ROSE ARBOR PLANTER ON PAGE 89

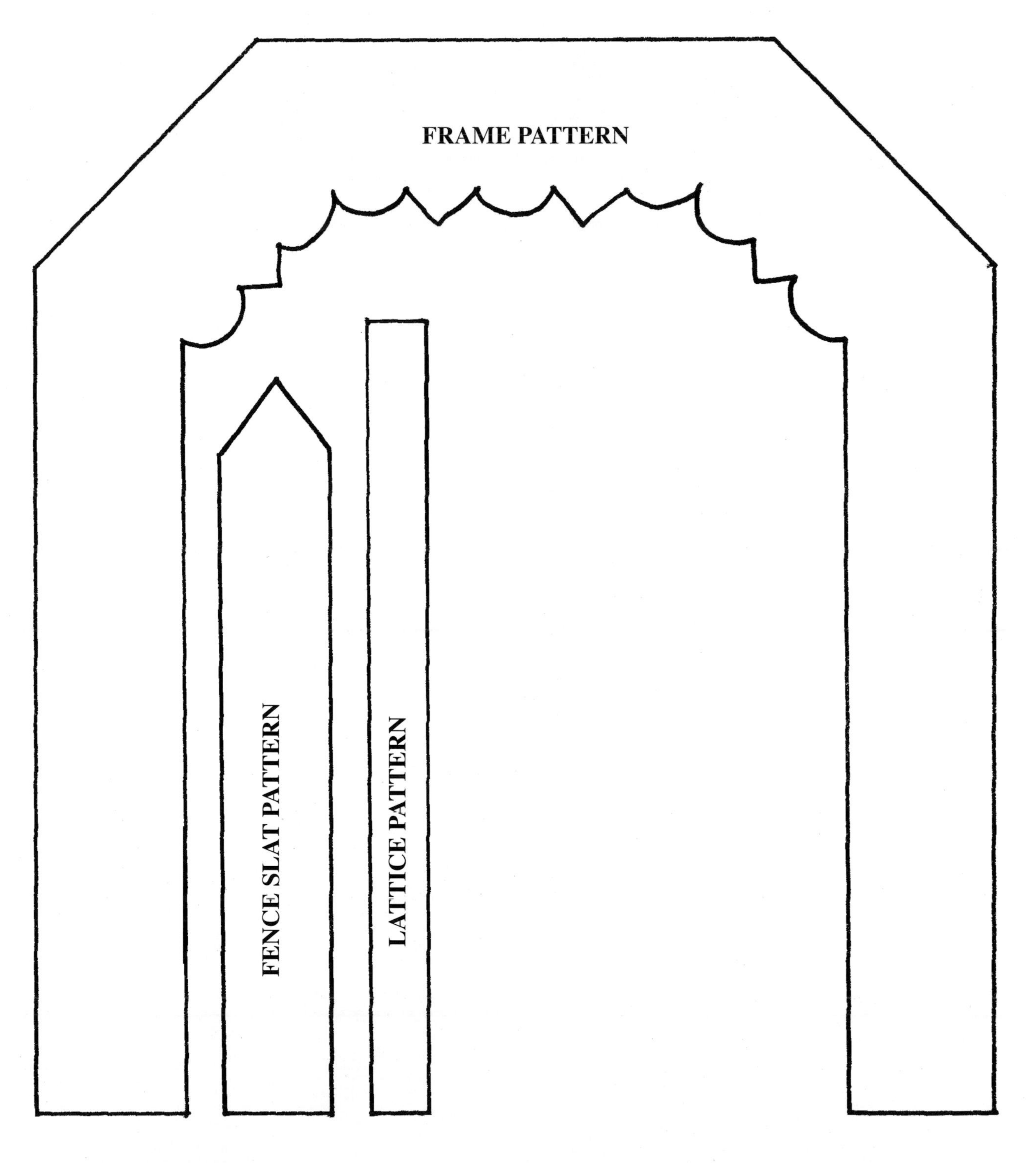

Rose Arbor Planter

Materials

One 15¼" x 10" piece of ¼" plywood
One 1" x 4" piece of pine wood, 34" long
Ten ¼" nails
White acrylic paint
Sealant
Wood glue

Tools

Jigsaw
Sandpaper
2" utility paintbrush
Hammer

Directions

1. Cut 1" x 4" pine into four 4" pieces. Also from pine, cut four 6" pieces.

2. Cut two 5¼" x 6" pieces of plywood.

3. Transfer rose arbor patterns to plywood, found on page 87; see "Tracing and Transferring" on page 8.

4. Cut out two frames, twelve fence slats, and thirteen lattice pieces.

5. Assemble two of the 4" pieces of pine as fronts and backs and two of the 6" pieces of pine as sides together to form a box. Secure box with nails at each joint.

6. Place one 5¼" x 6" plywood piece on bottom of box. Secure with nails.

7. Repeat Step 5 and 6 to make a second box.

8. Nail the frame to the two boxes, aligning inside edges of the frame with one side edge of each box; see photo.

9. Nail fence slats to the fronts of the boxes, six on each side of the frame; see photo.

10. Glue five lattice pieces to top of frame and four lattice pieces to sides of frame; see photo.

11. Apply sealant to planter.

12. Paint planter with white acrylic paint.

Window Flower Box

Materials

Three 6"-wide pieces of cedar fencing, 6 feet long
Two pieces of moulding, 8 feet long
One piece of smaller, rounded moulding, 8 feet long
Sixteen $1^1/_4$" wood screws
Two hooks
Twenty $1^1/_4$" nails
Twine
Gold acrylic paint
Wood glue

Tools

Tracing paper
Transfer paper
Jigsaw
Sandpaper
Exterior wood stain
2" utility paintbrush
Hammer

Directions

1. From large moulding, cut two 36" lengths and two 24" lengths with 45-degree ends.

2. From small moulding, cut two 24" lengths, two 11" lengths, and one $11^3/_4$" length.

3. From cedar fencing, cut two $40^1/_2$" lengths, two 5" lengths, and one 39" x 5" piece.

4. Trace and transfer heart and star patterns from the Trellis on page 59 onto remaining piece of cedar fencing; see "Tracing and Transferring" on page 8.

5. Cut out heart and star; see "Woodworking" on page 9.

6. Paint the heart and star with gold paint. Allow to dry.

7. Assemble large moulding pieces to form window box; see diagram. Secure with wood screws.

8. Glue the two 24" pieces of small moulding vertically in center of window box spaced $11^3/_4$" apart; see diagram.

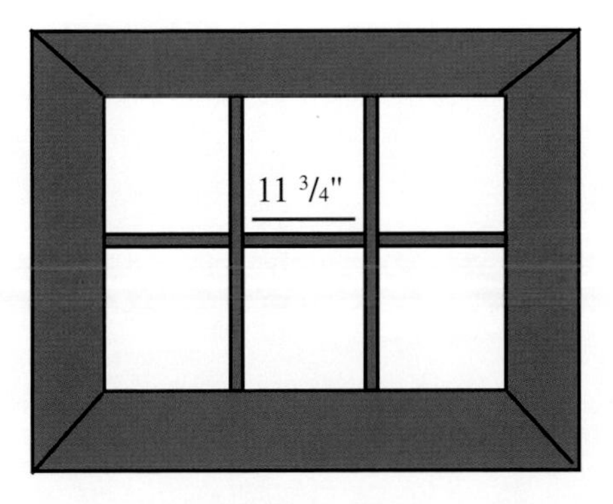

DIAGRAM

9. Glue the two 11" pieces of small moulding horizontally on each side of the vertical moulding.

10. Glue the remaining piece of small moulding between the vertical pieces of moulding.

11. Attach the two $40^1/_2$" lengths of cedar fencing to the two 5" lengths to form a box . Secure with two wood screws at each joint. Place the 39" x 5" piece inside box to form bottom; secure with a wood screw in each side.

12. Attach hooks to back of box.

13. Stain box with wood stain. Allow to dry.

14. Glue the heart and star to the front of the window box. Glue twine to heart and star.

15. Attach box to window frame with hooks on back of box.

Violets

Violet Tile Planter

Materials

One $15^1/_4$" x 10" piece of $^1/_4$" plywood
One 1" x 4" piece of pine wood, $38^1/_2$" long
Ten $^1/_4$" nails
One $^1/_4$" wooden dowel, 2" long
Assorted acrylic paints
Sealant
One 4-ounce kit of resin
Four paper cups
Wood glue

Tools

Jigsaw
Drill with $^1/_4$" drill bit
Sandpaper
2" utility paintbrush
Craft stick
Hammer

Directions

1. Cut 1" x 4" piece of pine into two $15^1/_4$" lengths and two 4" lengths.

2. Cut plywood into one $15^1/_4$" x $4^1/_2$" piece and four $3^1/_2$" squares.

3. Glue plywood squares onto one of the $15^1/_4$" lengths of pine for front; see Diagram A.

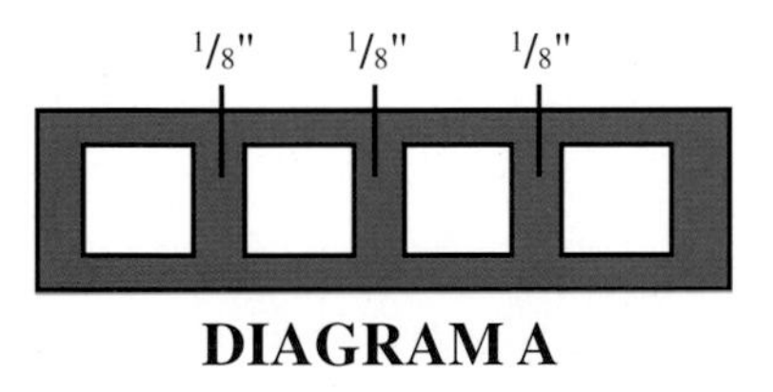

DIAGRAM A

4. Cut dowel into four $^1/_4$" pieces.

5. Drill four $^1/_4$"-deep holes into back of front piece; see Diagram B. Place dowels in holes.

DIAGRAM B

6. Drill two $^1/_4$"-deep holes into one side of each of the 4" lengths of pine; see Diagram C.

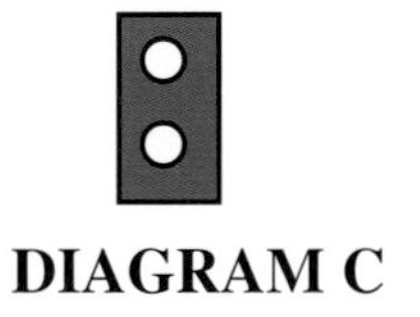

DIAGRAM C

7. Sand and apply sealant to front piece.

8. Paint lines on front, being careful to paint the sides of the tiles; see photo for color and placement. Allow to dry.

9. Paint the tiles; see photo for color and placement. Allow to dry. If desired, draw words or art on tiles with a permanent marker.

10. On a covered work space, place front piece right side up on paper cups to elevate.

11. Following manufacturer's instructions, pour resin over tiles. Level off with a craft stick, making sure entire board is covered. As resin drips, scrape it off the board with craft stick. Also, scrape between the tiles to create the look of grout. Continue scraping until resin drys. Let resin dry as directed in manufacturer's instructions.

12. Insert dowels on front piece into holes on sides, using wood glue to hold securely.

13. Attach $15^1/_4$" x $4^1/_2$" piece of plywood to bottom of box with nails.

Chapter Three
Autumn

ALL YOU
CAN
EAT

All-U-Can-Eat Fish

Materials

One 1" x 12" piece of pine, 3 feet long
Three 5/16"-diameter wooden dowels, 2 1/2" feet long
Sandpaper
Rust, yellow, light green, dark green, white, blue, orange, and black acrylic paint
Burnt umber artist's oil paint
Paint thinner
Oil-based varnish
Exterior varnish
Wood glue

Tools

Photocopy machine
Tracing paper
Transfer paper
Pencil
Jig saw
Drill with 1/4" bit
2"-wide utility paintbrush
1/4" flat artist's paintbrush
#2 round artist's liner brush
Hammer
Rags
Bowl or other small container to mix paint

Directions

1. Using a photocopy machine, enlarge Fish A pattern, found on page 98, 200%. Transfer enlarged fish pattern and all other fish patterns, found on page 99, to 1" x 12" pine; see "Tracing and Transferring" on page 8.

2. Using a jigsaw, cut out fish; see "Woodworking" on page 9.

3. Paint fish with appropriate base coats; refer to photo and pattern. Allow to dry.

4. Transfer details to painted fish; see "Tracing and Transferring" on page 8.

5. Paint details. Allow to dry.

6. Using drill, drill a hole in the bottom of each fish.

7. Put a dab of wood glue in each hole and insert dowels. Hammer in place if necessary.

8. Antique fish; see "Antiquing" on page 10.

9. Seal with exterior varnish.

Add a touch of whimsy to your lawn with these fish that are sure to bring a smile. Poking fun at the restaurant motto "All-U-Can Eat!", arrange the fish so that the largest fish is about to eat the middle fish, who is about to eat the littlest fish.

FISH A PATTERN

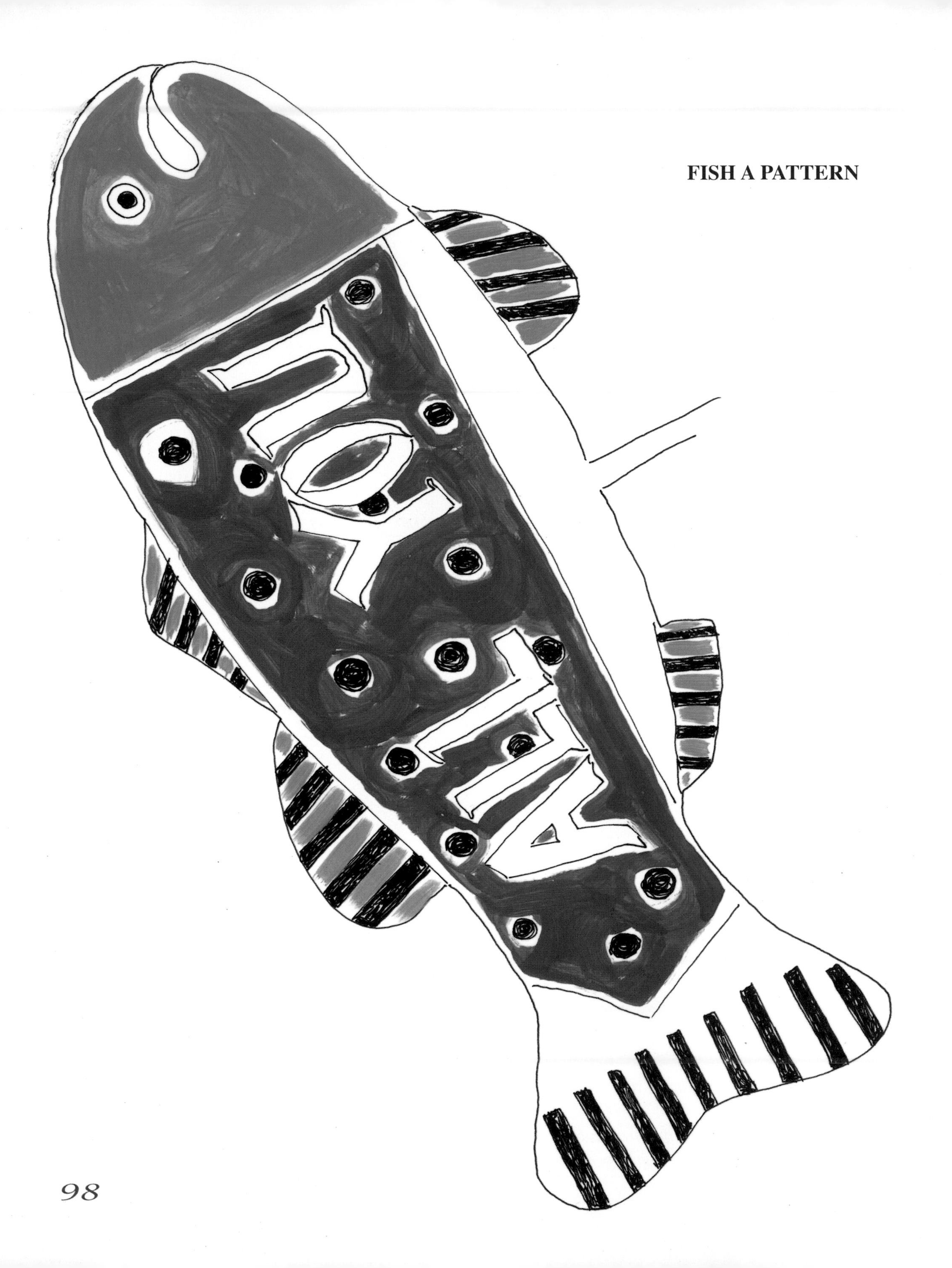

FISH PATTERNS

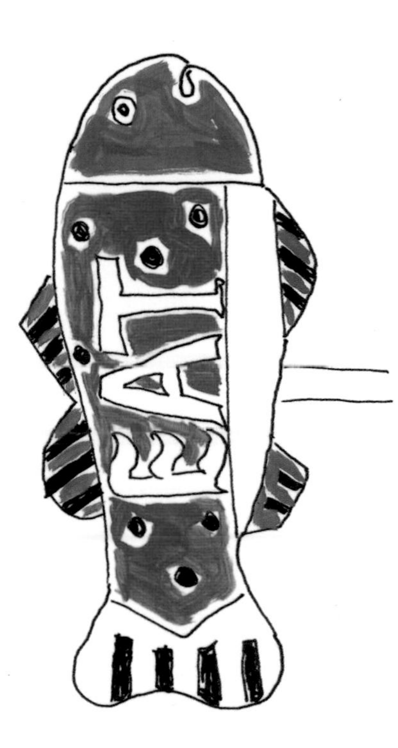

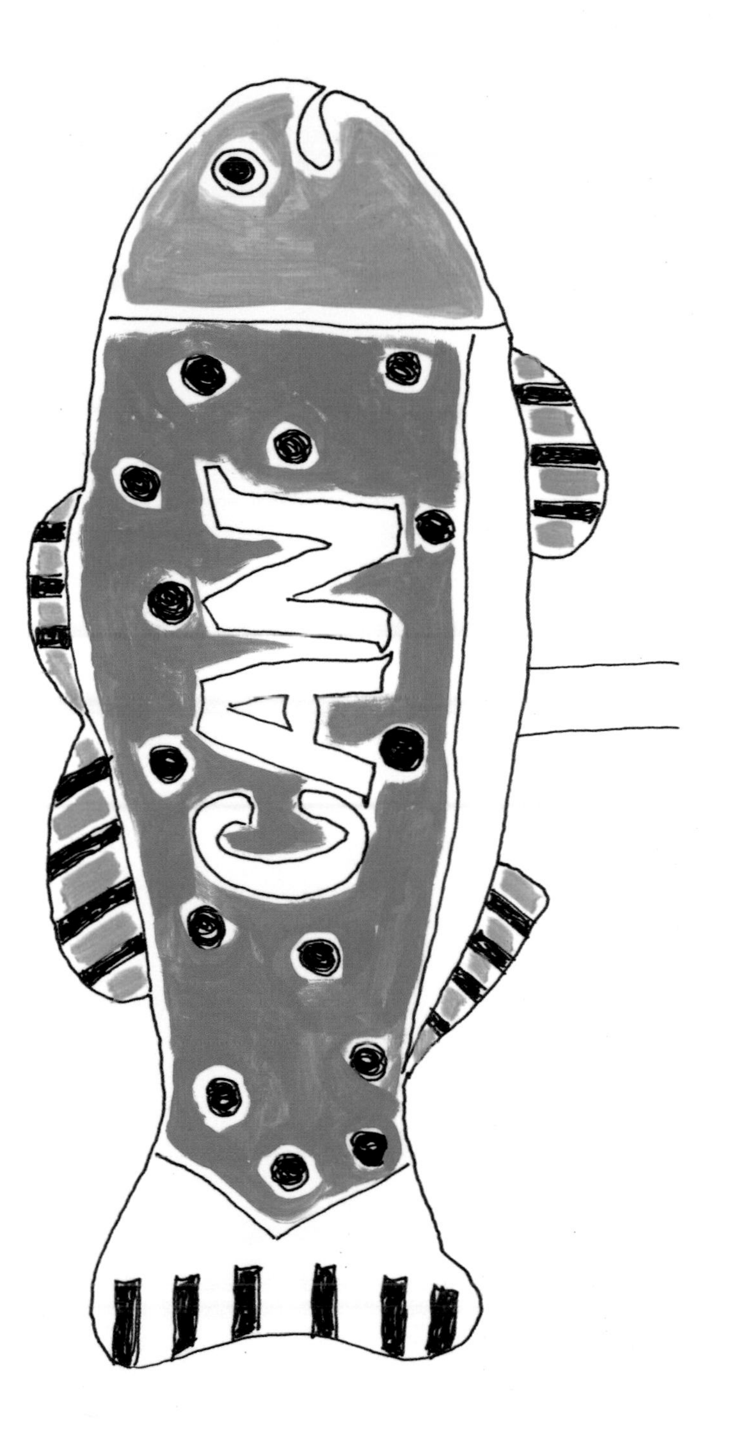

Frog Planter

Materials

One 1" x 12" piece of pine wood, 6 feet long
Twenty-four 1¼" wood screws
Wood putty
Dark green, light green, yellow, white, red, orange, and blue acrylic paint
Two small concrete frogs
Burnt umber artist's oil paint
Exterior varnish

Tools

Photocopy machine
Tracing paper
Transfer paper
Pencil
Table saw
Jigsaw
Phillips screwdriver or drill with screwdriver bit
Countersink bit
Putty knife
Tape measure
Sandpaper
2" utility paintbrush
¼" flat artist's brush
#2 round liner artist's brush
1" flat artist's brush

Directions

1. Cut three 24" x 5½" pieces of pine for box front, back, and bottom. Cut two 5½" x 4¾" pieces of pine for box sides; see "Woodworking" on page 9.

2. Trace and transfer pattern for end brackets and lily pads, found on page 102; see "Tracing and Transferring" on page 8.

3. Cut out four end brackets and two lily pads.

4. Lay out the pieces of the box as shown in the diagram. Attach the longer sides to the shorter sides with two wood screws at each joint. Be sure to predrill the screw hole locations with your countersink bit.

DIAGRAM

5. Attach bottom to the box with four countersunk screws running one through each side of the box.

6. Center and attach two brackets on one short side of box spaced 2" apart; secure with two wood screws in each bracket. Repeat on opposite side of box.

7. Attach lily pads to brackets with countersunk wood screws.

8. Putty and sand all countersunk screw locations.

9. Paint box with a base coat of dark green paint. Allow to dry.

10. Paint front side yellow, leaving a 1" border of dark green; see photo.

11. Using a photocopy machine, enlarge frog folk art pattern, found on page 102, 200%. Transfer enlarged pattern to front side of planter; see "Tracing and Transferring" on page 8.

12. Paint frog folk art; see photo and pattern for color and placement.

13. Seal with exterior varnish.

14. Set concrete frogs on lily pads.

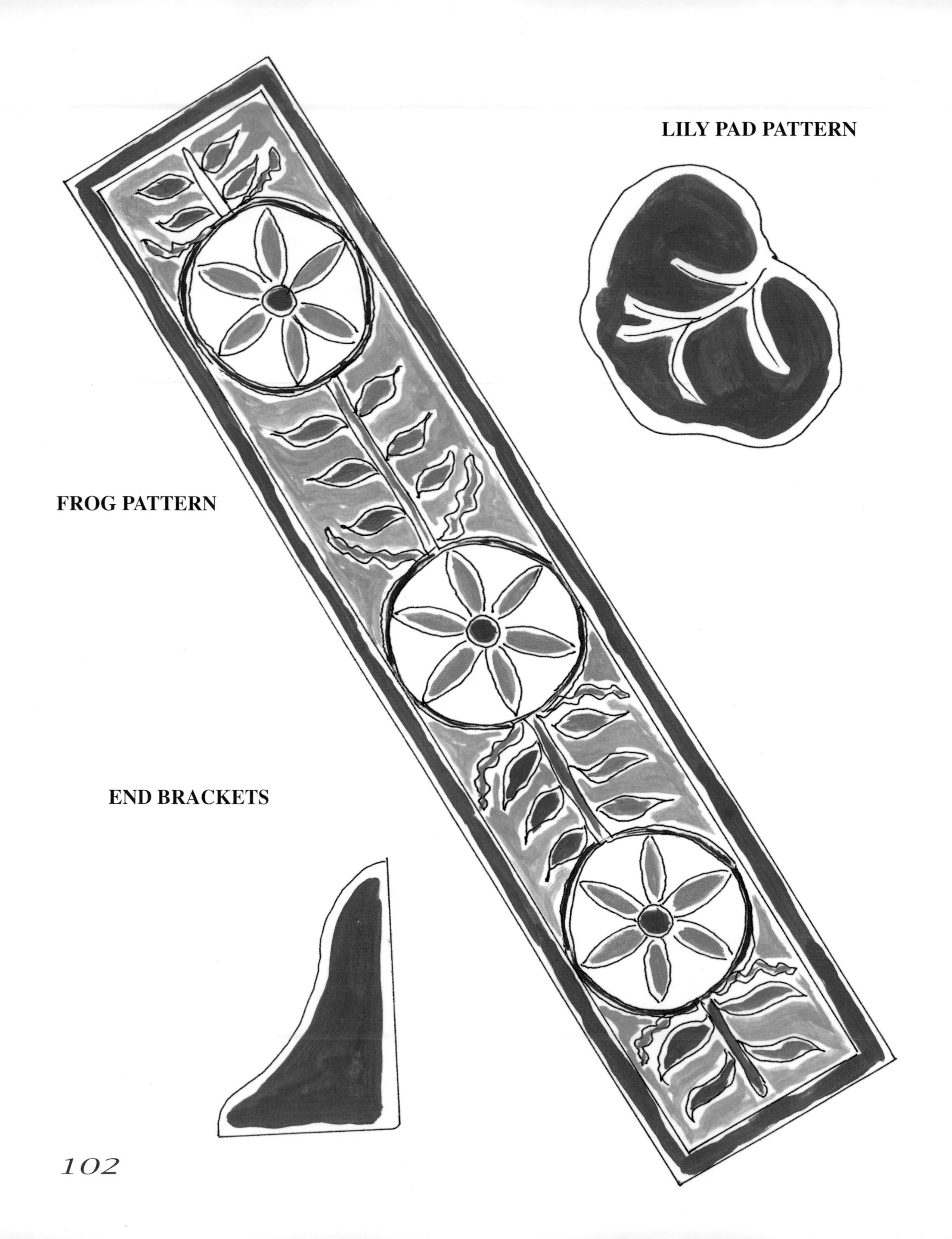
LILY PAD PATTERN
FROG PATTERN
END BRACKETS

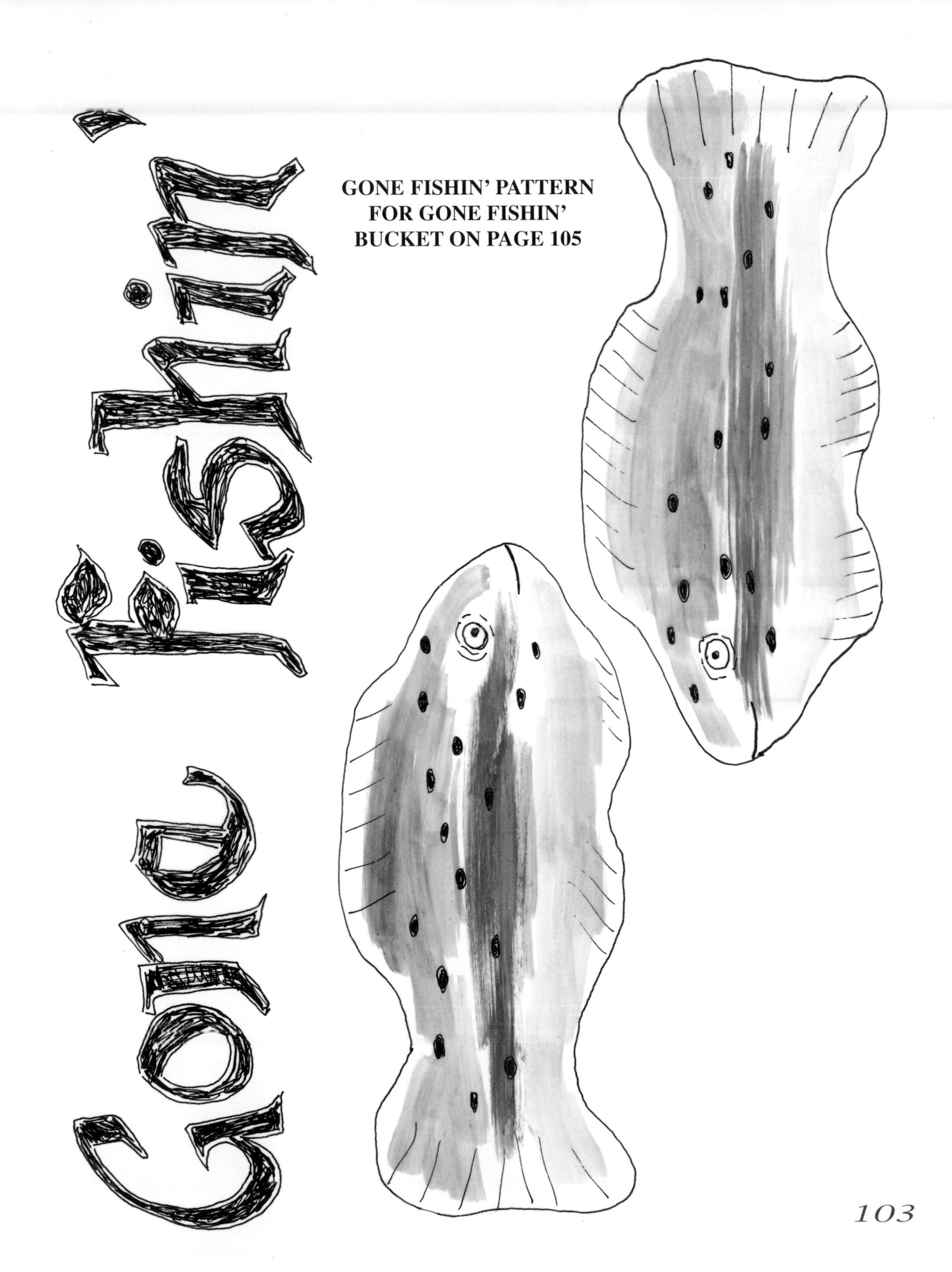

GONE FISHIN' PATTERN FOR GONE FISHIN' BUCKET ON PAGE 105

Gone Fishin

Gone Fishin' Bucket

Materials

One 13" metal bucket with handles
Exterior metal primer
Rust, olive green, yellow, and black acrylic paint
Burnt umber artist's oil paint
Paint thinner
Oil-based varnish
18" of 16 gauge wire
One 1" x 2" piece of pine wood, 2 feet long
One 1" x 12" piece of pine wood, 2 feet long
One 2" nail
Two small wood screws
Two brass swivel hooks (used to attach fishing lures)
12" of packaging twine

Tools

Tracing paper
Transfer paper
Pencil
Jigsaw
1" flat artist's brush
#2 round liner artist's brush
1/4" flat artist's brush
2" utility paintbrush
Rags
Bowl or small container to mix paint
Drill with 1/4" drill bit
Hammer

Directions

1. Trace and transfer fish pattern, found on page 103, to 1" x 12" pine; see "Tracing and Transferring" on page 8.

2. Cut out one fish. Using fish cutout as a pattern, cut out three more fish.

3. Paint fish with a base coat of olive green paint on the top of the fish, rust in the center of the fish, and yellow on the bottom of the fish. Allow to dry.

4. Trace and transfer details to fish; see "Tracing and Transferring" on page 8.

5. Paint details, referring to pattern.

6. Paint sign with a base coat of yellow. Allow to dry. Transfer and paint details; see "Tracing and Transfering" on page 8.

7. Antique fish, stake and sign; see "Antiquing" on page 10.

8. Paint the inside and outside of the bucket with exterior primer. Allow to dry.

9. Paint inside of bucket burgundy.

10. Paint outside of bucket dark green.

11. Drill two 1/4" holes in the top of the sign as indicated on pattern.

12. Wrap the wire around the sign through the holes.

13. Place a nail 2" from top of stake. Hang sign on nail.

14. Attach swivel to top of each fish with wood screws and hang on bucket handles.

15. Tie two fish together with packaging twine and hang from handles on bucket.

A touch of Huck Finn for your patio. The small rainbow trout are actually hung with swivel hooks fishermen use to tie lures to their line.

Tiled Wood Box

Materials

One 1" x 12" piece of pine wood, 3 feet long
Twelve 2" wood screws
Wood putty
Peach acrylic paint
Burnt umber artist's oil paint
Paint thinner
Oil-based varnish
Three 4" x 4" ceramic tiles
Exterior glue or exterior tile adhesive
Two 18" lengths of $^{3}/_{8}$"-diameter rope
Exterior varnish

Tools

Table saw
Phillips screwdriver or drill with Phillips drill bit
Countersink bit
Putty knife
Drill with $^{1}/_{2}$" drill bit
Sandpaper
2" utility paintbrush

Directions

1. Cut three 18" x $5^{1}/_{2}$" pieces of pine for box front, back, and bottom. Cut two $4^{3}/_{4}$" x $5^{1}/_{2}$" pieces for box sides; see "Woodworking" on page 9.

2. Lay out the pieces of the box as shown in the diagram. Attach the longer sides to the shorter sides with two wood screws at each joint. Be sure to predrill the screw hole locations with your countersink bit.

DIAGRAM

3. Attach bottom to the box with four countersunk screws running one through each side of the box.

4. Putty and sand all countersunk screw locations.

5. Paint box peach. Allow to dry.

6. Antique box; see "Antiquing" on page 10.

7. Drill two $^{1}/_{2}$" holes through both short sides of box.

8. Thread one 18" length of rope through holes on one side of box, knotting rope on the inside of the box to secure. Repeat on opposite side with remaining length of rope.

9. Center and glue tiles to front of box.

10. Seal with exterior varnish.

11. Adjust handles to desired size.

Decorative tiles come in a wide variety of colors and patterns and make a great accent on a planter. Create a coordinated look by matching tiles with existing surroundings.

Scarecrow

Materials

One 1" x 12" piece of pine wood, 10 feet long
One 2" x 4" piece of pine wood, 10 feet long
One piece of 2" x 4" pine wood, 6 feet long
Light blue, red, white, orange, green, black, tan, and brown acrylic paint
Twelve yards of packaging twine
Burnt umber artist's oil paint
Paint thinner
Oil-based varnish
Exterior varnish
Ten 1¼" wood screws

Tools

Photocopy machine
Tracing paper
Transfer paper
Pencil
Jigsaw
Wood clamps
Sandpaper
Drill with ¼" drill bit
#2 Phillips screwdriver or drill with #2 Phillips screw bit
2" utility paintbrush
¼" flat artist's brush
#2 round artist's liner brush
Rags
Scissors
Bowl or other small container to mix paint
Concrete mix (optional)

Directions

1. Using a photocopy machine, enlarge scarecrow patterns, found on pages 110 and 111, 400%. Transfer enlarged patterns to 1" x 12" pine; see "Tracing and Transferring" on page 8.

2. Cut out the scarecrow; see "Woodworking" on page 9.

3. Paint scarecrow; see pattern and photograph for colors and placement. Allow to dry.

4. Transfer details; see "Tracing and Transferring" on page 8.

5. Paint details. Allow to dry.

6. Antique scare crow; see "Antiquing" on page 10.

7. Drill holes in scarecrow; see pattern for placement.

8. Join scarecrow parts together, tying twine through drilled holes; leave enough slack so that parts will bend.

9. To make stake, attach the 6-foot length of pine to the 10-foot length of pine, 12" from the top; secure with wood screws.

10. Secure the head and body of the scare crow to the stake with wood screws.

11. Bury the stake far enough in the ground so that the scarecrow is stable. You may need to secure the stake in concrete for additional support.

12. To pose the scar crow, secure the arms and legs with additional twine.

This scarecrow is a charming addition to your lawn or garden. On his arm is a whirligig found on page 113. Since this scarecrow is jointed like a puppet, he can be posed with string.

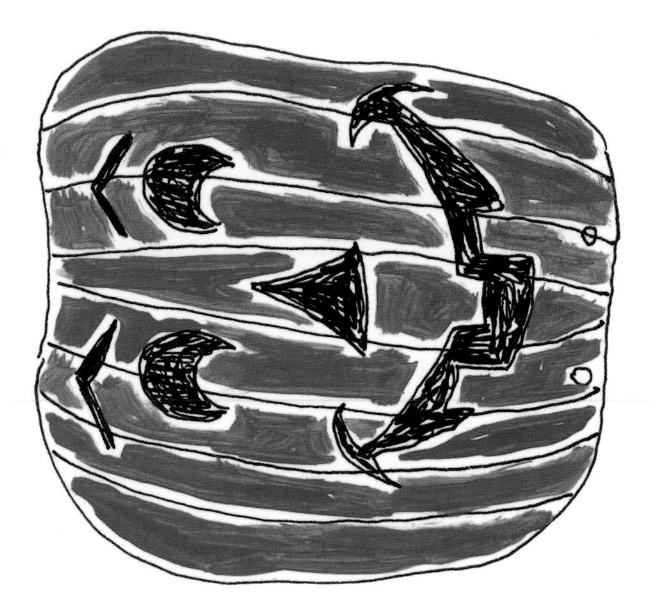

SCARECROW PATTTERNS

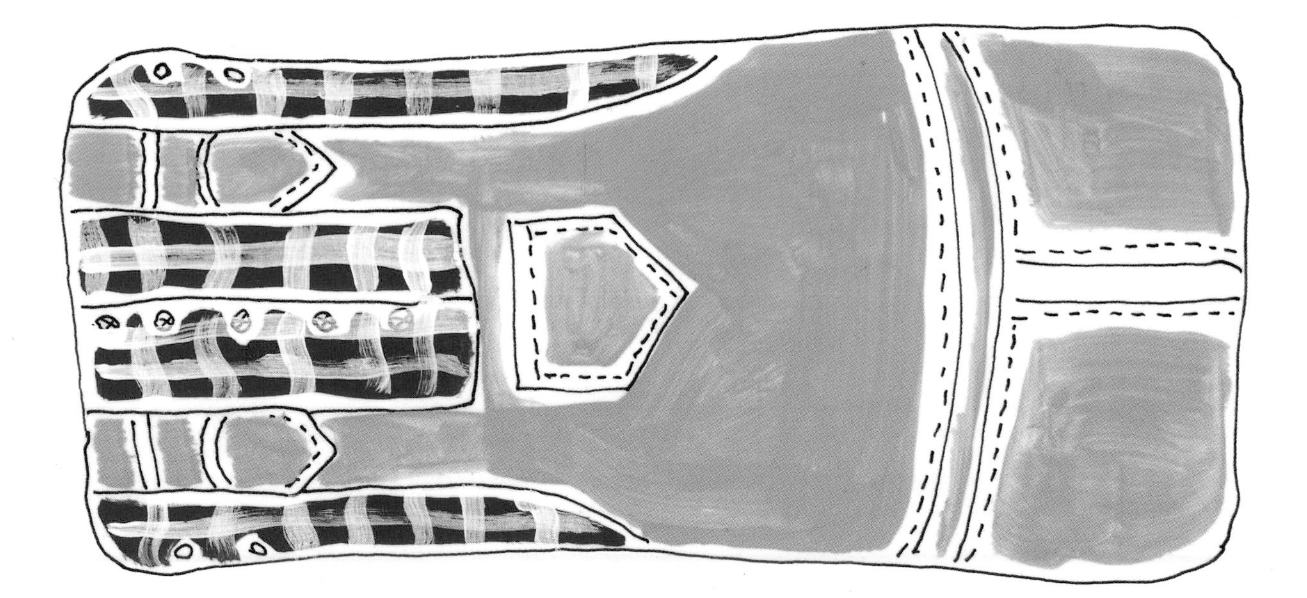

SCARECROW PATTERNS

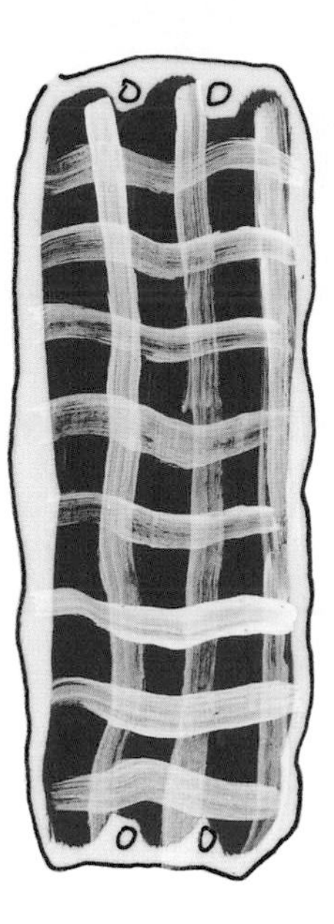

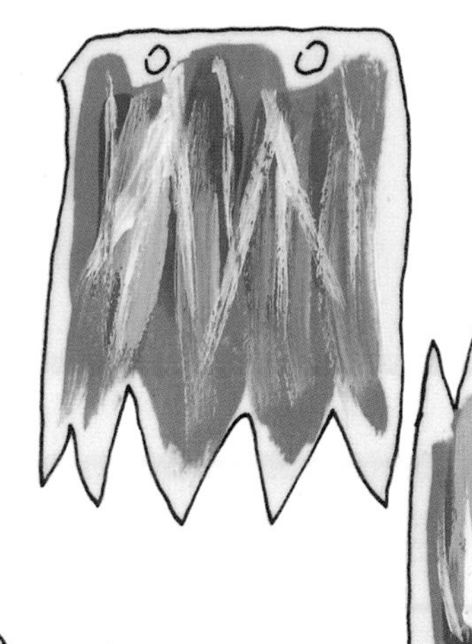

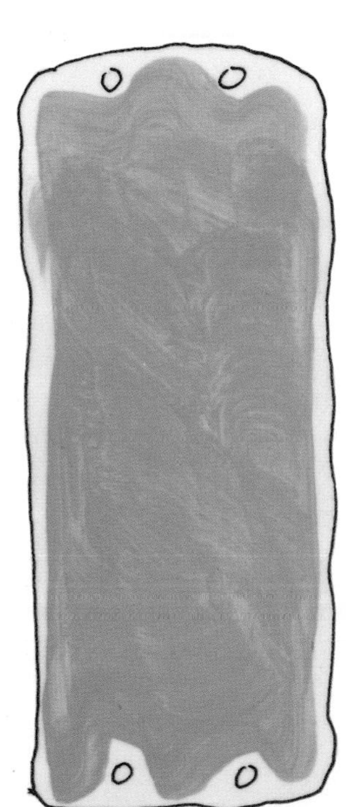

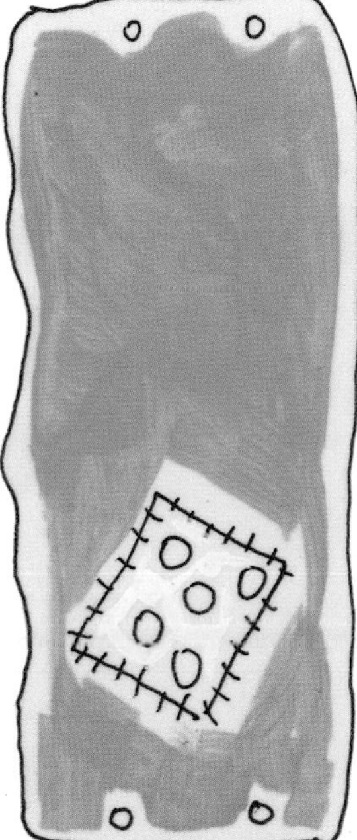

Whirligig

Materials

One 1" x 12" piece of pine wood, 1 foot long
Black, white, and yellow acrylic paint
8" length of 5/16"-diameter wooden dowel
Two 9" black toy airplane propellers
Two 1 1/4" long flat-heat nails (head must be larger than hole at center of propellers)
Two 1/4" plastic spacers
Exterior varnish
Nail polish remover

Tools

Tracing paper
Transfer paper
Pencil
Jigsaw
Wood clamps
Sandpaper
1" flat artist's brush
1/4" flat artist's brush
Drill with a 1/4" drill bit
Hammer

Directions

1. Trace and transfer yard bird pattern from page 20 to 1" x 12" pine; see "Tracing and Transferring" on page 8.

2. Cut out bird; see "Woodworking" on page 9.

3. Paint bird with a base coat of black paint. Allow to dry.

4. Paint beak and dowel yellow. Paint eye white with a black center. Allow to dry.

5. Drill a 1/4" hole 1/2" deep in bottom of bird.

6. Insert dowel and hammer in place.

7. Remove names from propeller with nail polish remover or paint propellers to match bird's body.

8. Put nail through propeller, then through 1/4" spacer. Hammer into place on sides of bird; see photo. Spacer will keep the propeller from hitting the bird's body and enable it to spin freely.

9. Attach bird to arm of Scarecrow on page 109.

10. Seal with exterior varnish.

Whirligigs can be very complicated and require advanced woodworking skills and patience to get the wings to work in the wind. Prefabricated toy propellers make this project easy.

Pumpkins

Materials

- One piece of 1" x 12" pine wood, 8 feet long
- Six pieces of 1" x 1" pine, 18" long
- Orange, black, and tan acrylic paint
- 72" of 16 gauge black annealed tie wire
- 18" of 1/2"-diameter wooden dowel
- Burnt umber artist's oil paint
- Paint thinner
- Oil-based varnish
- Twelve 1 1/4" wood screws
- Exterior varnish
- Wood glue

Tools

- Photocopy machine
- Tracing paper
- Transfer paper
- Pencil
- Jigsaw
- Wood clamps
- Sandpaper
- 2" utility paintbrush
- 1/4" flat artist's brush
- #2 round artist's liner brush
- Wire cutters
- Rags
- Bowl or other small container to mix paint
- #2 Phillips screwdriver or drill with #2 Phillips screw bit
- Drill with a 1/16" drill bit

Directions

1. Using a photocopy machine, enlarge pumpkin patterns, found on pages 116 and 117, 200%. Transfer enlarged patterns to 1" x 12" pine; see "Tracing and Transferring" on page 8.

2. Cut out pumpkins; see "Woodworking" on page 9.

3. Paint pumpkins with a base coat of orange paint. Allow to dry.

4. Transfer details; see Tracing and Transferring" on page 8.

5. Paint details. Allow to dry.

6. Antique pumpkins; see "Antiquing" on page 10.

7. Cut 1/2" dowels into six 3" lengths.

8. Paint dowels tan.

9. Glue dowels on top of each pumpkin to form stems.

10. Cut twelve 6" lengths of wire.

11. Paint wires tan.

12. Drill two 1/16" holes on each side of stems.

13. Coil each length of wire around a pencil or similar object to form tendrils. Remove pencil and glue wire in holes.

14. Cut one end of each 1" x 1" piece of pine at a diagonal to form stake; see diagram.

DIAGRAM

15. Attach one stake to the back of each pumpkin with wood screws.

16. Seal with exterior varnish.

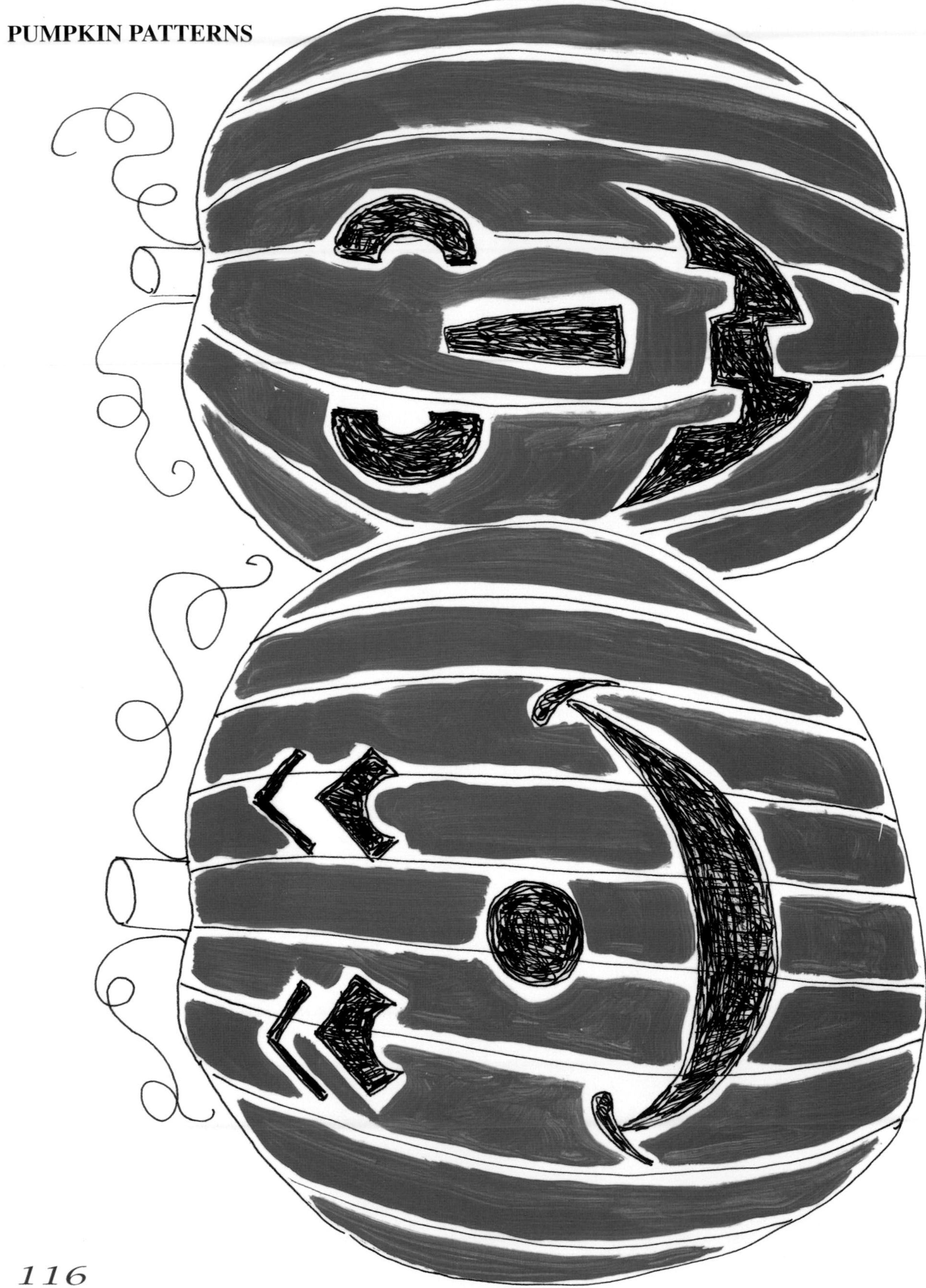

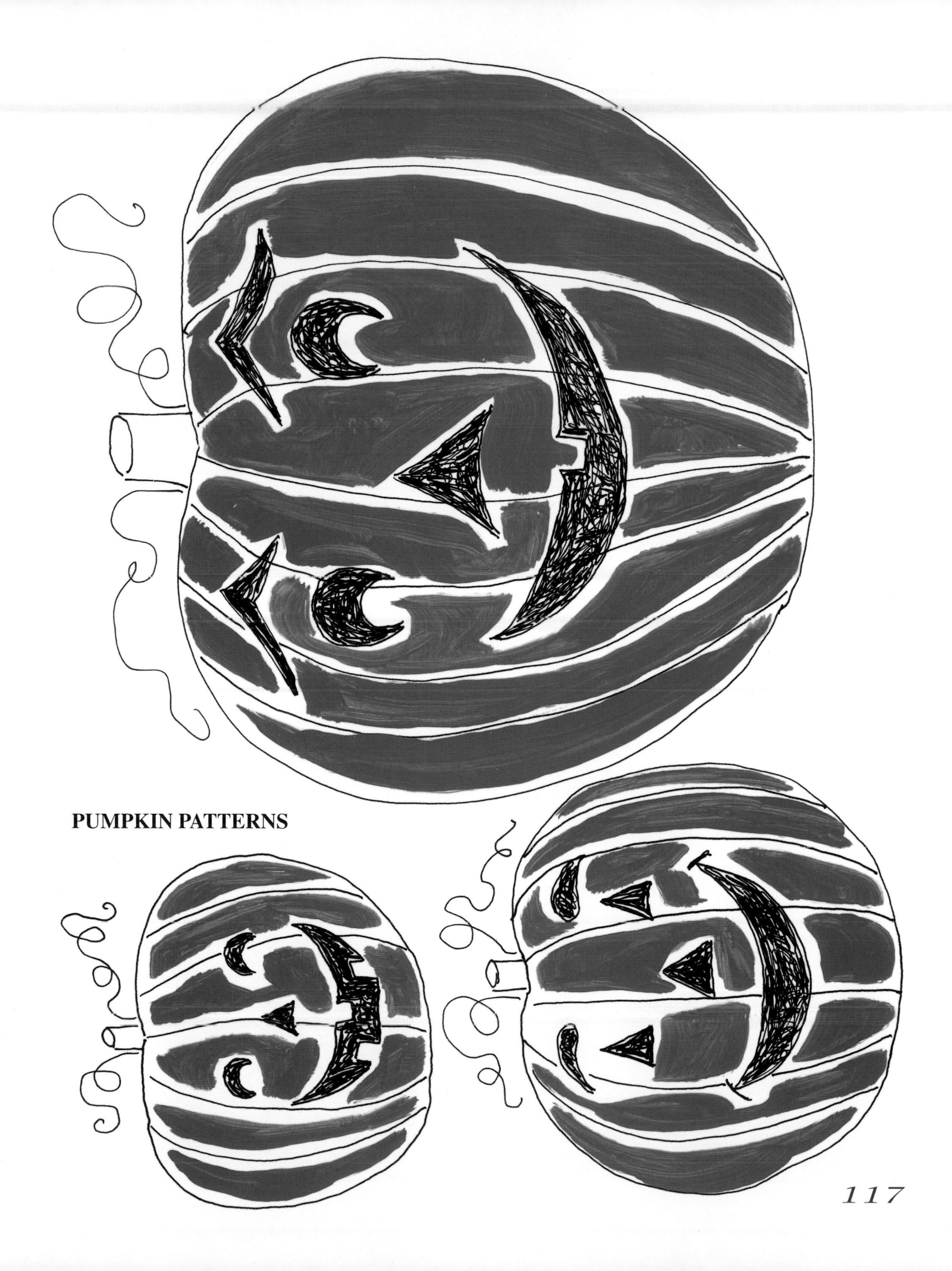

PUMPKIN PATTERNS

Bronzed Concrete Pot

Materials

One 20"-diameter concrete pot with embossed designs
Dark brown water-based wood stain
Turquoise, rust, and orange acrylic paint
Bronze rub-on metallic wax
Exterior varnish

Tools

2" utility paintbrush
Rags
Bowl or small container to mix paint

Directions

1. Working small areas at a time, brush pot with water-based wood stain, wiping off excess. Allow to dry. The stain will make tiny cracks in the cement stand out, adding to its antique look.

2. Dilute a small amount of turquoise paint 1:1 with water.

3. Working small areas at a time, brush pot with diluted turquoise paint, wiping off excess. Allow to dry.

4. Highlight raised designs and edges with rub-on metallic wax.

5. Accent pot with small amounts of rust paint in a few areas to simulate a rusted effect. Allow to dry.

6. Seal with exterior varnish.

Easily turn brand-new concrete pots into antique bronze pots you might find in a Grecian garden.

Fence Pot Shelf

Materials

One 2" unfinished wooden shelf
Red, white, and green acrylic paint
Exterior varnish
Three 4"-diameter terra-cotta pots

Tools

2" utility paintbrush
Tracing paper
Transfer paper
Pencil
1/4" flat artist's brush

Directions

1. Paint shelf red.

2. Paint upper rim of pots with a base coat of white paint.

3. Trace and transfer ivy pattern to pots; see "Tracing and Transferring" on page 8.

4. Paint ivy, referring to photo and pattern for color and placement.

5. Seal with exterior varnish.

6. Place pots on shelf.

IVY PATTERN

An easy solution to a bland fence ajoining the patio—a fence shelf pot holder. A purchased shelf and pot make it super easy, or try painting your own pot with the included ivy pattern.

Chapter Four

Winter

Patina Banded Pots

Materials

Two terra-cotta-colored plastic pots with embossed bands
White, turquoise, tan, green, metallic copper, and black acrylic paint
Exterior varnish

Tools

2" utility paintbrush
1" flat artist's paintbrush
Rags
Bowl or small container to mix paint

You can hardly believe these were plastic pots that you can get most anywhere. With a little paint, they look like expensive copper-banded terra-cotta pots. In minutes you can create a mottled, uneven color that naturally takes years to achieve, taking that artificial plastic look away completely. The copper band complements the effect beautifully.

Directions

1. Dilute a small amount of white acrylic paint 1:1 with water.

2. Brush diluted paint mixture onto a small section of pot and wipe off excess with rag, leaving an uneven haze or wash of color. The paint dries quickly, so do not paint an area larger than you can work with before it dries. Allow to dry.

3. Brush tan paint over white painted pot, wiping off excess as in Step 2. Allow to dry.

4. Repeat Step 3 with green and turquoise paint. Allowing paint to dry between coats.

5. Paint embossed band black and patina; see General Instructions for "Copper Patina" on page 11.

6. Seal with exterior varnish.

HERBS
HERBS

Herb Planter

Materials

One 1" x 12" piece of pine wood, 3 feet long
Four 2½"-diameter terra-cotta pots
Acetate transparency
Green and white acrylic paint
Wood putty
Exterior varnish

Tools

Photocopy machine
Tracing paper
Transfer paper
Table saw
Compass
Putty knife
Drill with ¼" drill bit
Jigsaw
Phillips screwdriver or a drill with Phillips screw bit
2" utility paintbrush
Craft knife or single-edge razor
Small sponge
⅛" flat artist's brush

Directions

1. Cut one 11¼" x 11¼" piece of pine for top. Cut two 3" x 11¼" pieces of pine for front and back, and two 3" x 9¾" pieces of pine for sides.

2. Using a compass, mark four 2" holes, centered on top piece. Space centers 5½" from each other; see diagram.

DIAGRAM

3. Cut out holes; see "Woodworking" on page 9.

4. Lay out the pieces of the box as shown in the diagram. Attach the longer sides to the shorter sides with two wood screws at each joint. Be sure to predrill the screw hole locations with your countersink bit.

5. Attach the top to the box with four countersunk screws running through each side of the box.

6. Putty and sand all countersunk screw locations.

7. Paint planter with a base coat of green paint. Allow to dry.

8. Trace "Herbs" ; see "Tracing and Transferring on page 8. Using a photocopy machine, copy pattern onto an acetate transparency.

9. Cut out letters with a craft knife or razor blade.

10. Using sponge, stencil pattern onto each side of planter with white acrylic paint. Allow to dry.

11. Using a small paintbrush, replace the centers of the letters "R" and "B" with green paint.

12. Seal with exterior varnish.

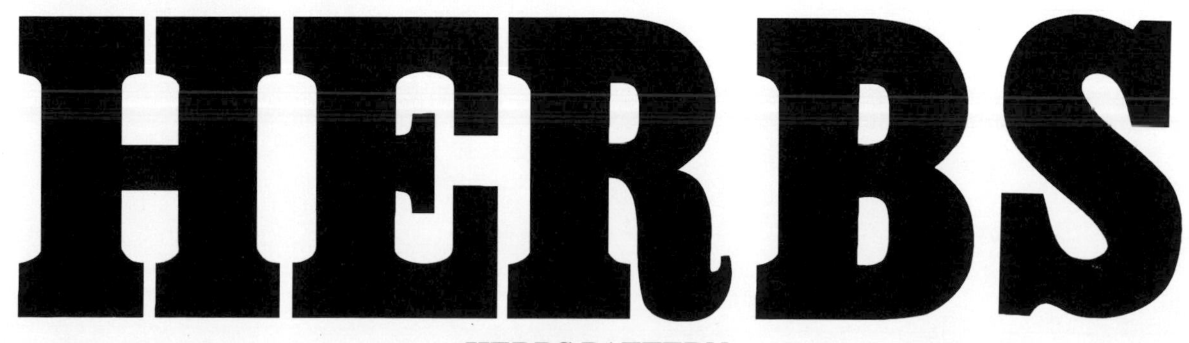

HERBS PATTERN

Gold Leaf Pots

Materials

One 6"-tall terra-cotta pot
One 4"-tall terra-cotta pot
One package of gold leaf
Spray adhesive
Exterior varnish

Tools

Small paintbrush

Directions

1. Since terra-cotta pots are naturally a reddish-brown color, there is no need to paint them first.

2. Apply gold leaf to outside of pots.

3. Seal with exterior varnish.

Flower pots can be decorated in a variety of ways for the holidays. Try silver or bronze leafing in place of the gold leafing, try painting the pot a base coat of deep red and antiquing with gold or bronze paint, or try painting the pot a neutral base color and adding poinsettias, holly, or pinecones and acorns.

Plastic Laminate Planter

Materials

One piece of 1" x 12" redwood, 3 feet long
Sixteen 1¼" wood screws
One 11½" x 15" x ¾" piece of exterior grade plywood
One 30" x 18" piece of plastic laminate (Formica)
Contact cement glue
13 feet of 1"-wide flat moulding trim
Wood putty
Walnut exterior wood stain
Wood glue

Tools

Table saw
Phillips screwdriver or drill with Phillips screw bit
Drill and countersink bit
Sandpaper
Putty knife
Heavy-duty scissors or craft knife
Measuring tape
2" utility paintbrush

Directions

1. Using a table saw, cut redwood into two 15" x 5" pieces for box front and back. Cut two pieces 10" x 5" for sides.

2. Lay out the pieces of the box as shown in the diagram. Attach the longer sides to the shorter sides with two wood screws at each joint. Be sure to predrill the screw hole locations with your countersink bit.

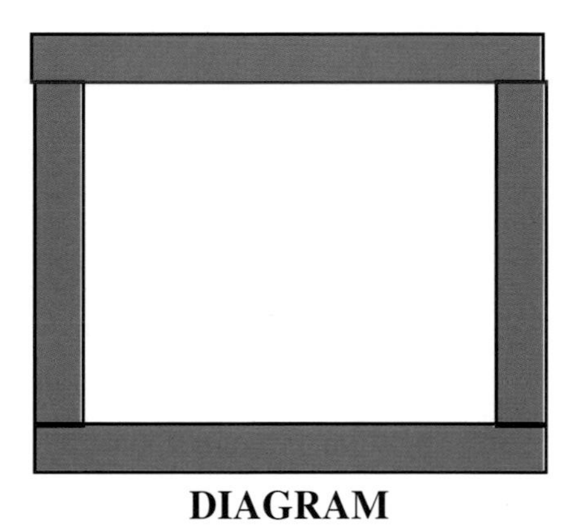

DIAGRAM

3. Attach the plywood piece to the bottom of the box with four countersunk screws running through each side of the box.

4. Putty and sand all countersunk screw locations.

5. Cut plastic laminate slightly smaller than each side. Glue in place with contact cement glue; see photo for placement.

6. Cut moulding strips to trim the box top, bottom, and corners, beveling ends at a 45-degree angle for corners.

7. Stain inside of box and moulding pieces. Allow to dry.

8. Glue moulding strips in place with wood glue.

Plastic laminate comes in a variety of colors, textures, and patterns. The plastic laminate on this planter creates a metallic effect. A different look would be obtained depending on which type you choose.

Grape Pot

Materials

One 14"-diameter terra-cotta pot with embossed grapes and grapevine
Two dozen assorted plastic gem stones
Purple, white, light green, and dark green acrylic paint
White artist's oil paint
Paint thinner
Oil-based varnish
Exterior varnish

Tools

1" flat artist's brush
1/4" flat artist's brush
2" utility paintbrush
Hot glue gun with glue sticks
Bowl or small container to mix paint
Rags

This jeweled grape pot will dress up any patio. Old buttons or jewelry would also work on this project.

Directions

1. Paint grapes purple. Paint leaves and vines light green and dark green. Allow to dry.

2. Glue gem stones at random to outer side of pot.

3. Using white paint, antique pot with a whitewash; see "Antiquing" on page 10.

4. Seal with exterior varnish.

Patina Buckets

Materials

One 9"-diameter galvanized bucket
One 11"-diameter galvanized bucket
One 12" x 12" piece of 36-gauge tooling copper
2 yards of 16-gauge wire
Flat black spray paint
Turquoise and metallic copper acrylic paint
Exterior varnish

Tools

Tracing paper
Pencil
Tin snips or old scissors
Wire cutters
2" utility paintbrush
Bowl or small container for mixing paint
Rags
Hot glue gun and glue sticks

Directions

1. Trace leaf pattern; see "Tracing and Transferring" on page 8. Place pattern on top of tooling copper and retrace pattern. This will leave an imprint of the leaf.

2. Repeat, tracing five leaves onto tooling copper.

3. Cut out leaves with tin snips.

4. Paint and patina leaves and buckets; see "Copper Patina" on page 11.

5. Bend one end of leaf around handle of one bucket and hot-glue to secure.

6. Repeat, hot gluing two or three leaves to each handle.

7. Cut wire into varying lengths. Coil wire around a pencil or similar object to form tendrils. Remove pencil and twist wires around handles of buckets.

8. Seal with exterior varnish.

SLED PATTERNS FOR SLED ON PAGE 137

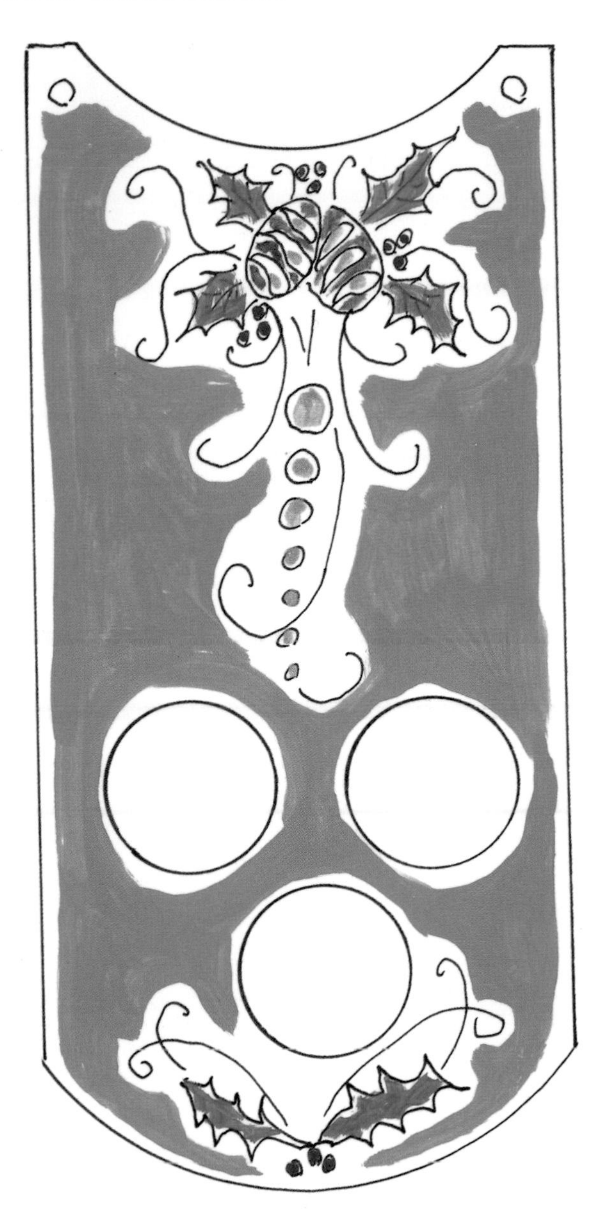

Sled Planter

Materials

One 1" x 12" piece of pine, 8 feet long
1 quart of blue exterior acrylic paint
Brown, white, dark green, red, gold, metallic gold, and black acrylic paint
Six 1¼" wood screws
Wood putty
Burnt umber artist's oil paint
Paint thinner
Oil-based varnish
Exterior varnish
48" of ½"-diameter gold cord
Three 5"-diameter terra-cotta pots

Tools

Photocopy machine
Tracing paper
Transfer paper
Pencil
Jigsaw
Sandpaper
Drill with ¾" bit
Countersink bit
Wood clamps
Putty knife
2"-wide utility paintbrush
¼" flat artist's brush
1" flat artist's brush
#2 round artist's liner brush
Rags
Bowl or small container to mix paint
Scissors or knife

Directions

1. Using a photocopy machine, enlarge sled patterns, found on page 135, 400%. Transfer enlarged patterns to 1" x 12" pine; see "Tracing and Transferring" on page 8.

2. Using jigsaw, cut out sled pieces; see "Woodworking" on page 9. Using side runner cutout as a pattern, cut out an additional side runner.

3. Sand edges of wood if necessary.

4. Transfer the three circles to top piece of sled; see "Tracing and Transferring" on page 8.

5. Cut out the three circles; see "Woodworking" on page 9.

6. Transfer rope holes to the top end of the sled.

7. Drill ¾" holes in top end of sled.

8. On each side of top, drill three holes, one at each end and one in the middle, with countersink bit.

9. Attach top to sides with wood screws through countersunk holes.

10. Fill countersunk holes with putty. Allow to dry. Sand smooth.

11. Paint entire sled with blue paint. Allow to dry.

12. Transfer details to top and sides; see "Tracing and Transferring" on page 8.

13. Paint details. Allow to dry.

14. Antique; see "Antiquing" on page 10.

15. Seal with exterior varnish. Allow to dry.

16. For handle, thread rope through holes in side pieces, knotting ends to hold in place.

17. Place terra-cotta pots in hole in top of sled.

Santa

Materials

One piece of 1" x 12" pine wood, 13 feet long
One piece of 1" x 2" pine wood, 5 1/2 feet long
1 quart of burgundy flat acrylic paint
Reddish-brown, white, pinkish-flesh tone, light blue, black, metallic gold, and dark green acrylic paint
Spray adhesive
One package of gold leaf
Burnt umber artist's oil paint
Paint thinner
Oil-based varnish
Twenty 1 1/4" wood screws
One 1 1/2" utility hinge with screws
Exterior varnish

Tools

Photocopy machine
Tracing paper
Transfer paper
Pencil
Jigsaw
Wood clamps
2" utility paintbrush
1" flat artist's brush
1/4" flat artist's brush
#2 round liner artist's brush
Bowl or small container to mix paint
Rags
Drop cloth
Hot glue gun and glue sticks
Phillips screwdriver or drill with Phillips bit
Drill with 1/4" bit

Directions

1. Using a photocopy machine, enlarge Santa patterns, found on pages 140 and 141, 400%. Transfer enlarged patterns to 1" x 12" pine; see "Tracing and Transferring" on page 8.

2. Cut out pattern pieces; see "Woodworking" on page 9. You will need two upper arm pieces, two lower arm pieces, and four cuff trim pieces.

3. Paint beard and mustache white.

4. Paint coat trim pieces reddish-brown. Allow to dry.

5. Gold-leaf trim pieces; see "Gold Leafing" on page 11.

6. Transfer details for body, arms, face, and coat; see "Tracing and Transferring" on page 8. Do not transfer details of face, holly on coat, and reindeer before painting these pieces with the appropriate base coat.

7. Paint coat and entire back of body, upper arms, and lower arms burgundy. Paint face flesh. Paint mittens black. Refer to patterns and photo for color and placement. Allow to dry.

8. Transfer details of face and coat; see "Tracing and Transferring" on page 8.

9. Paint details, referring to pattern and photo for colors and placement. Allow to dry.

10. Antique all pieces, including piece of 1" x 2" pine; see "Antiquing" on page 10.

11. Glue two cuff trim pieces to each arm; see photo for placement.

12. Attach center coat trim piece to front of body with wood screws from back side.

13. Glue the bead and mustache pieces in place; see photo.

14. Join upper arm to lower arm with wood screws, posing as desired.

15. Attach the piece of 1" x 2" to the back of the head with the utility hinge for stand.

16. Drill a 1/4" hole in upper part of the arm to hold greenery; see photo.

17. Seal with exterior varnish.

SANTA PATTERNS

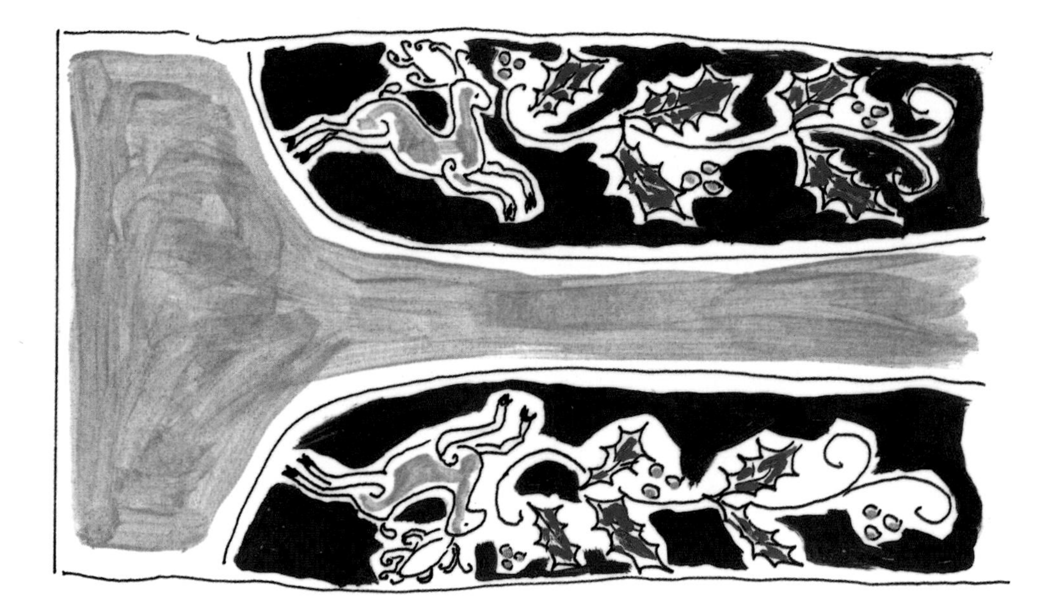

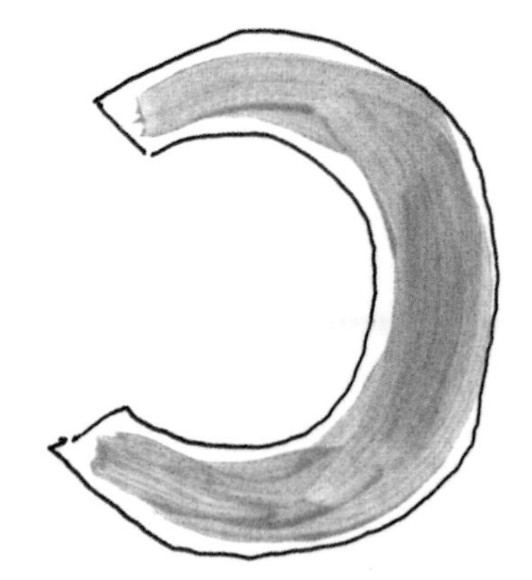

SANTA PATTERNS

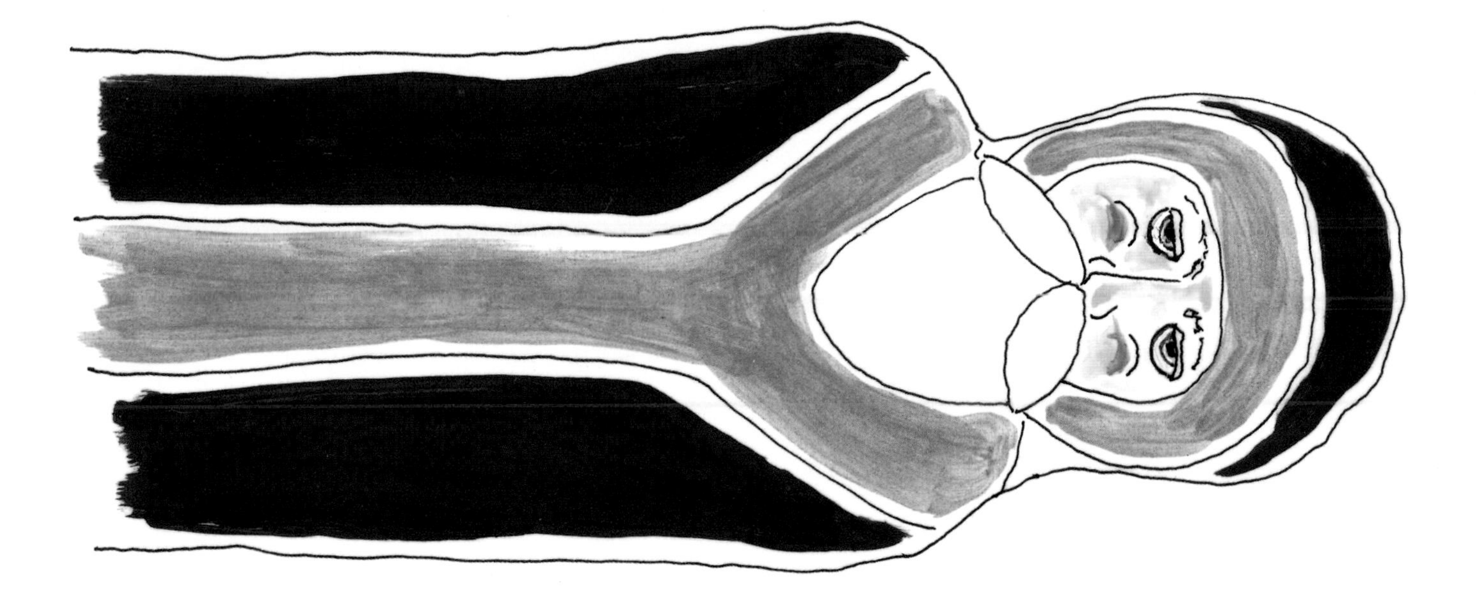

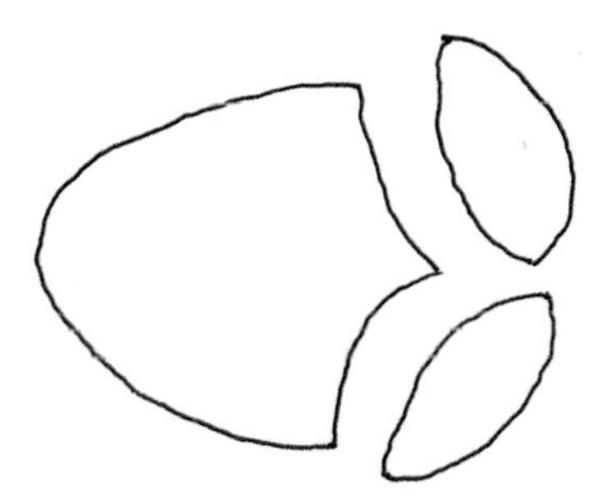

Metric Equivalence Chart

MM-Millimetres   CM-Centimetres

INCHES TO MILLIMETRES AND CENTIMETRES

INCHES	MM	CM	INCHES	CM	INCHES	CM
1/8	3	0.9	9	22.9	30	76.2
1/4	6	0.6	10	25.4	31	78.7
3/8	10	1.0	11	27.9	32	81.3
1/2	13	1.3	12	30.5	33	83.8
5/8	16	1.6	13	33.0	34	86.4
3/4	19	1.9	14	35.6	35	88.9
7/8	22	2.2	15	38.1	36	91.4
1	25	2.5	16	40.6	37	94.0
1 1/4	32	3.2	17	43.2	38	96.5
1 1/2	38	3.8	18	45.7	39	99.1
1 3/4	44	4.4	19	48.3	40	101.6
2	51	5.1	20	50.8	41	104.1
2 1/2	64	6.4	21	53.3	42	106.7
3	76	7.6	22	55.9	43	109.2
3 1/2	89	8.9	23	58.4	44	111.8
4	102	10.2	24	61.0	45	114.3
4 1/2	114	11.4	25	63.5	46	116.8
5	127	12.7	26	66.0	47	119.4
6	152	15.2	27	68.6	48	121.9
7	178	17.8	28	71.1	49	124.5
8	203	20.3	29	73.7	50	127.0

YARDS TO METRES

YARDS	METRES	YARDS	METRES	YARDS	METRES	YARDS	METRES	YARDS	METRES
1/8	0.11	2 1/8	1.94	4 1/8	3.77	6 1/8	5.60	8 1/8	7.43
1/4	0.23	2 1/4	2.06	4 1/4	3.89	6 1/4	5.72	8 1/4	7.54
3/8	0.34	2 3/8	2.17	4 3/8	4.00	6 3/8	5.83	8 3/8	7.66
1/2	0.46	2 1/2	2.29	4 1/2	4.11	6 1/2	5.94	8 1/2	7.77
5/8	0.57	2 5/8	2.40	4 5/8	4.23	6 5/8	6.06	8 5/8	7.89
3/4	0.69	2 3/4	2.51	4 3/4	4.34	6 3/4	6.17	8 3/4	8.00
7/8	0.80	2 7/8	2.63	4 7/8	4.46	6 7/8	6.29	8 7/8	8.12
1	0.91	3	2.74	5	4.57	7	6.40	9	8.23
1 1/8	1.03	3 1/8	2.86	5 1/8	4.69	7 1/8	6.52	9 1/8	8.34
1 1/4	1.14	3 1/4	2.97	5 1/4	4.80	7 1/4	6.63	9 1/4	8.46
1 3/8	1.26	3 3/8	3.09	5 3/8	4.91	7 3/8	6.74	9 3/8	8.57
1 1/2	1.37	3 1/2	3.20	5 1/2	5.03	7 1/2	6.86	9 1/2	8.69
1 5/8	1.49	3 5/8	3.31	5 5/8	5.14	7 5/8	6.97	9 5/8	8.80
1 3/4	1.60	3 3/4	3.43	5 3/4	5.26	7 3/4	7.09	9 3/4	8.92
1 7/8	1.71	3 7/8	3.54	5 7/8	5.37	7 7/8	7.20	9 7/8	9.03
2	1.83	4	3.66	6	5.49	8	7.32	10	9.14

Index

About the Author

Edie Stockstill is an artist and designer. For many years she has designed, manufactured, and marketed a line of American and European folk art pieces based on historical research. These include wood pieces, decoys, carousel horses, and canvases, as well as privately commissioned pieces.

When she is not painting, she enjoys gardening and working in the yard, as well as hiking, skiing, and biking with her family in the mountains and canyons of Utah.